Title: "Voices of Freedom: A Journey through Human Rights"

This book, along with its contents encompassing text, illustrations, images, diagrams, and other creative elements, is the exclusive property of FAISAL JAMIL and is safeguarded by copyright law.

FAISAL JAMIL asserts full ownership and retains all rights to this book. No part of this publication may be reproduced, distributed, or transmitted in any form or by any means, such as photocopying, recording, or electronic methods, without prior written consent from the copyright holder. Brief quotations in critical reviews and certain noncommercial uses permitted by copyright law are exceptions.

This copyright notice applies to all editions, formats, and translations of the book, whether in print, digital, or any other medium or technology existing now or developed in the future. Unauthorized use or infringement may result in legal action and pursuit of remedies under applicable copyright laws.

While efforts have been made to ensure accuracy and reliability, FAISAL JAMIL does not guarantee the completeness or suitability of the information. Readers are responsible for evaluating and using the content judiciously.

FAISAL JAMIL reserves the right to make changes, updates, or corrections to the book without prior notice. Inclusion of third-party materials or references does not imply endorsement or affiliation unless used under fair use principles or with proper permissions and attributions.

For permissions, inquiries, or requests regarding the book's use, please contact FAISAL JAMIL through official channels listed on their Amazon author page or provided email address.

Warm regards,

FAISAL JAMIL

I Always Give's Free Copies Need Your Feedback And

Reviews Keeps In Touch!

http://www.amazon.com/author/faisal.jamil

Email: faisaljamilauthor@gmail.com

About the author

Certainly! Faisal Jamil is a multifaceted individual with a diverse set of skills and experiences. With a strong foundation in computer knowledge since childhood, he has developed a deep understanding of technology that informs his work as a content writer. Faisal also possesses digital skills, which further enhance his abilities in various digital platforms and technologies.

Beyond his professional endeavors, Faisal Jamil has also excelled in the martial arts, particularly Shotokan Karate, where he achieved the prestigious rank of first Dan black belt. This achievement speaks to his dedication, discipline, and commitment to personal growth and mastery.

In his professional life, Faisal Jamil has carved out a successful career in sales management within the Fast Moving Consumer Goods (FMCG) sector. His roles in various FMCG companies have honed his skills in strategic planning, team leadership, and business development. Faisal's ability to drive sales and achieve targets has been instrumental in his career progression, showcasing his talent for identifying opportunities and delivering results.

Faisal Jamil is also deeply interested in business investment strategies, planning, and execution. His understanding of these areas has been key to his success in the business world, allowing him to make informed decisions and implement effective strategies. His ability to navigate the complexities of investment planning and execution has set him apart as a strategic thinker and a valuable asset in any business endeavor.

Overall, Faisal Jamil is a dynamic individual who combines his passion for technology, martial arts, sales management, digital skills, and business investment strategies to achieve success in diverse fields. His journey is a testament to his versatility, resilience, and continuous pursuit of excellence.

Yours Sincerely

FAISAL JAMIL

I Always Give's Free Copies Need Your Feedback And

Reviews Keeps In Touch!

https://www.amazon.com/author/faisal.jamil

Email: faisaljamilauthor@gmail.com

VOICES OF FREEDOM
A JOURNEY THROUGH
HUMAN RIGHTS

Table of Content

Preface

In an era where the concept of human rights is both celebrated and contested, *Voices of Freedom: A Journey through Human Rights* seeks to illuminate the profound and enduring struggle for justice, dignity, and equality. This book is born out of a deep conviction that understanding the history, principles, and ongoing efforts in the field of human rights is crucial to fostering a more just and equitable world.

Human rights are not abstract ideals confined to legal texts or international declarations; they are the lived experiences of individuals and communities striving for recognition, respect, and fairness. From the ancient civilizations that laid the groundwork for our modern understanding to the pivotal moments in history that shaped the human rights landscape, this journey is a testament to the resilience and courage of countless individuals who have fought for their rights and the rights of others.

As you embark on this journey through the pages of this book, you will encounter stories of remarkable individuals who have risked everything to stand up against oppression and injustice. Their voices, echoing through the corridors of history, remind us that the fight for human rights is far from over. It is a continuous process that requires our collective effort, empathy, and unwavering commitment.

Each chapter of this book delves into a specific facet of human rights, providing a comprehensive exploration of the issues, struggles, and triumphs that have defined this field. From civil and political rights that protect our freedoms to economic, social, and cultural rights that ensure our well-being, from the rights of children to the rights of indigenous peoples, this book covers a broad spectrum of human rights topics, offering insights and real-life examples that bring these concepts to life.

In writing *Voices of Freedom*, our goal was to create a resource that is both informative and inspiring. We aimed to provide a balanced perspective that acknowledges the complexities and challenges in the human rights arena while celebrating the progress and victories that have been achieved. We hope that this book will serve as a source of knowledge, motivation, and empowerment for readers of all backgrounds.

The journey through human rights is one that involves not only understanding the past but also envisioning a better future. As you read through the chapters, you will see the emerging issues and challenges that lie ahead, and the innovative solutions and advocacy efforts that are shaping the future of human rights. It is our hope that this book will inspire you to become an active participant in the ongoing quest for justice and equality.

We are deeply grateful to the many individuals and organizations whose tireless work and dedication to human rights have made this book possible. Their stories and contributions are the heartbeat of this book, and their unwavering commitment to human dignity and justice is a source of inspiration for us all.

Finally, we dedicate this book to all those who have fought, and continue to fight, for human rights. May their courage and determination light the way for future generations, and may their voices of freedom resonate loudly and clearly across the globe.

With hope and solidarity,

FAISAL JAMIL

INTRODUCTION

Welcome to *Voices of Freedom: A Journey through Human Rights*. This book is a testament to the enduring and universal struggle for human dignity, justice, and equality. Human rights, the fundamental freedoms and protections to which every person is entitled, have evolved through centuries of conflict, advocacy, and transformation. This journey is far from over, and understanding its past, present, and future is essential to shaping a world where everyone can live freely and with dignity.

In this book, we embark on a comprehensive exploration of human rights, beginning with their historical origins and progressing through the significant milestones, challenges, and triumphs that have defined their evolution. Each chapter delves into a specific aspect of human rights, shedding light on the principles, struggles, and victories that have brought us to where we are today.

A Glimpse into the Past:

The Birth of Human Rights

We start our journey with the ancient civilizations and key historical documents that laid the groundwork for modern human rights. From the Magna Carta to the Enlightenment, these early foundations have shaped our understanding of justice and liberty.

The Universal Declaration of Human Rights: A Turning Point

In 1948, the world witnessed a monumental step forward with the adoption of the Universal Declaration of Human Rights (UDHR). This document, born out of the ashes of World War II, set forth a common standard of rights for all people. We'll explore the significance of the UDHR, the key players involved, and its enduring impact on global human rights advocacy.

Civil and Political Rights: Safeguarding Individual Freedoms

Civil and political rights are essential to protecting individual freedoms. These rights, including freedom of speech, assembly, and the right to a fair trial, are the cornerstones of democratic societies. Through real-life stories, we'll see how individuals and movements have fought for these freedoms, often at great personal risk.

Economic, Social, and Cultural Rights: Ensuring Human Dignity

The right to work, education, and an adequate standard of living are crucial for human dignity. We'll examine how these rights contribute to well-being and equality, sharing examples of efforts to ensure that everyone can lead a fulfilling life.

The Right to Equality and Non-Discrimination:

A Universal Struggle

Equality and the fight against discrimination based on race, gender, religion, and other factors are fundamental human rights issues. We'll highlight landmark cases and movements that have advanced equality, demonstrating the ongoing struggle to achieve a just society.

The Rights of Children:

Protecting the Most Vulnerable

Children have specific rights that need special attention. From the right to education to protection from exploitation, we'll explore how these rights are essential for the development and well-being of children worldwide.

Women's Rights:

A History of Resilience and Empowerment

The struggle for women's rights has been long and arduous. We'll examine key issues such as voting rights, equal pay, and reproductive rights, spotlighting the influential women leaders who have driven progress.

Indigenous Peoples' Rights:

Preserving Culture and Identity

Indigenous peoples possess unique rights that respect their cultural heritage and connection to the land. We'll share stories of indigenous communities' fight for recognition, justice, and cultural preservation.

The Right to Health:

Access and Equity

Healthcare is a fundamental right, yet access remains uneven globally. We'll discuss the right to health, global health issues, and initiatives aimed at improving health outcomes for all.

The Right to Education:

Building a Brighter Future

Education is a powerful tool for empowerment and change. We'll explore efforts to improve access to quality education and how education can transform lives and communities.

Freedom of Expression and Information:

The Pillars of Democracy

The right to freely express opinions and access information is vital for democracy. We'll highlight the role of the media, the internet, and the challenges faced by journalists and activists.

The Right to Privacy:

Navigating the Digital Age

In our increasingly digital world, the right to privacy is more important than ever. We'll examine issues such as data protection, surveillance, and the balance between security and privacy.

The Right to Work and Fair Conditions:

Dignity in Labor

Fair labor conditions are essential for human dignity. We'll discuss issues like minimum wage, safe working environments, and the fight against forced and child labor.

Environmental Rights:

Protecting Our Planet for Future Generations

Environmental rights are emerging as a crucial area of human rights. We'll explore the impact of climate change and pollution on human rights and the importance of environmental justice.

Refugees and Asylum Seekers:

Seeking Safety and Dignity

Refugees and asylum seekers face immense challenges. We'll highlight their rights and share stories of individuals and families seeking safety, emphasizing the need for compassion and justice.

Human Rights in the Digital Age:

New Frontiers and Challenges

Technology is transforming human rights. We'll explore digital freedom, cyberbullying, and the right to internet access, discussing both the opportunities and threats posed by technological advancements.

The Role of International Organizations:

Guardians of Human Rights

International organizations play a vital role in promoting and protecting human rights. We'll examine the contributions of entities like the United Nations, Amnesty International, and Human Rights Watch.

Human Rights Defenders:

Courage in the Face of Adversity

Human rights defenders risk their lives for justice and equality. We'll celebrate their bravery and dedication, sharing inspiring stories of activists who stand up against oppression.

Challenges and Controversies:

Navigating the Present and Future

The human rights field is fraught with challenges and controversies. We'll discuss issues such as balancing security and freedom, the impact of global crises, and the need for continued vigilance and innovation.

The Future of Human Rights:

A Vision for Tomorrow

In our final chapter, we'll reflect on the future of human rights. We'll discuss emerging issues, potential solutions, and the importance of continued advocacy and education to build a more just and equitable world.

Conclusion:

A Call to Action

As we conclude this journey through human rights, we invite you to join the global movement for justice, equality, and dignity. Every voice matters, and together, we can create a future where the principles of human rights are universally respected and upheld.

Voices of Freedom: A Journey through Human Rights aims to inspire, educate, and empower readers to understand and advocate for human rights. Through stories of resilience, courage, and determination, we hope to highlight the importance of these fundamental rights and the collective efforts needed to protect and promote them for all.

Chapter 1
The Birth of Human Rights

Introduction: The Concept of Human Rights

Begin with an explanation of what human rights are: the basic rights and freedoms that belong to every person in the world, from birth until death. These rights apply regardless of where you are from, what you believe, or how you choose to live your life. They can never be taken away, although they can sometimes be restricted.

Ancient Civilizations and Early Ideas of Rights

Discuss how early ideas of justice, fairness, and rights can be traced back to ancient civilizations.

Mesopotamia:

The Code of Hammurabi (circa 1754 BCE) is one of the earliest known sets of laws. Although not human rights as we understand them today, these laws established rules and consequences, promoting a form of social order and justice.

Greece:

The concept of democracy originated in Athens. Philosophers like Socrates, Plato, and Aristotle discussed justice, the role of the individual in society, and the idea of natural law.

Rome:

Roman law introduced ideas about citizenship and the rights of citizens, influencing later legal systems. The Roman Republic also established early forms of representative government.

The Influence of Religious and Philosophical Thought

Explain how religious and philosophical traditions contributed to the development of human rights concepts.

Christianity:

Emphasized the inherent worth of every individual, the concept of charity, and the moral responsibility to treat others with respect and dignity.

Islam:

The Quran and Hadiths outline principles of justice, equality, and the welfare of all members of the community, including women and non-Muslims.

Confucianism:

Stressed the importance of respect, duty, and the welfare of the people.

Hinduism and Buddhism:

Promoted ideas of compassion, respect for all living beings, and the importance of moral actions.

Medieval Developments

Discuss the evolution of human rights concepts during the medieval period.

Magna Carta (1215):

This English charter was one of the first documents to put into writing the principle that the king and his government were not above the law. It granted certain rights to nobles and, over time, influenced the development of the rule of law and constitutionalism.

The Renaissance and Humanism:

Focused on the value and potential of the individual. Thinkers like Erasmus and Thomas More challenged the authority of the church and monarchy, advocating for more personal freedom and responsibility.

The Enlightenment: A Revolution in Thought

Explain how the Enlightenment period in the 17th and 18th centuries significantly advanced the concept of human rights.

John Locke:

Argued for the natural rights to life, liberty, and property. His ideas about government by consent and the right to rebellion against unjust rulers influenced many later thinkers and political movements.

Jean-Jacques Rousseau:

Advocated for the social contract and the idea that legitimate government authority comes from the consent of the governed.

Voltaire:

Championed freedom of speech and religion, criticizing intolerance and oppression.

Montesquieu:

His work on the separation of powers influenced the development of modern democratic governance.

Key Documents and Milestones

Highlight significant documents that laid the groundwork for modern human rights.

The English Bill of Rights (1689):

Limited the powers of the king and established certain civil liberties, such as the right to a fair trial and protection against cruel and unusual punishment.

The American Declaration of Independence (1776):

Asserted the right to life, liberty, and the pursuit of happiness. It emphasized that governments are instituted to secure these rights, deriving their just powers from the consent of the governed.

The French Declaration of the Rights of Man and of the Citizen (1789):

Proclaimed the equality of all men, the sovereignty of the people, and the protection of natural rights.

Conclusion: The Foundations of Modern Human Rights

Summarize how these historical developments laid the foundations for modern human rights. Emphasize the gradual evolution of these ideas, influenced by various cultures, religions, and philosophies, leading to the comprehensive frameworks we have today.

Transition to the next chapter, which will discuss the creation and impact of the Universal Declaration of Human Rights in 1948, marking a significant milestone in the global recognition and protection of human rights.

Chapter 2
The Universal Declaration of Human Rights

Introduction: The Post-War Context

Begin by setting the historical context. After the devastation of World War II, there was a global recognition of the need to establish a framework to protect human rights and prevent such atrocities from occurring again. The horrors of the Holocaust and the widespread violations of human rights during the war highlighted the necessity for a universal standard.

The Formation of the United Nations

Explain the creation of the United Nations in 1945, emphasizing its primary goal of promoting peace, security, and cooperation among countries. The UN Charter included the promotion of human rights as a fundamental objective.

The Commission on Human Rights

Introduce the establishment of the Commission on Human Rights in 1946, chaired by Eleanor Roosevelt. This commission was tasked with drafting a document that would articulate the rights and freedoms to which all humans are entitled.

Key Figures Involved

Eleanor Roosevelt:

As the chairperson of the commission, she played a pivotal role in driving the process and ensuring diverse perspectives were included.

René Cassin:

A French jurist who was instrumental in drafting the declaration, later receiving the Nobel Peace Prize for his work.

John Humphrey:

A Canadian scholar who prepared the initial draft of the declaration.

Charles Malik:

A Lebanese philosopher and diplomat who contributed significantly to the philosophical and ethical dimensions of the declaration.

Peng Chun Chang:

A Chinese philosopher who emphasized the inclusion of cultural diversity and Confucian principles.

Drafting the Declaration

Describe the process of drafting the Universal Declaration of Human Rights (UDHR). Over two years, extensive discussions and negotiations took place, involving representatives from various cultural, religious, and political backgrounds. The aim was to create a document that reflected universal values and principles.

Adoption by the General Assembly

Detail the adoption of the UDHR by the United Nations General Assembly on December 10, 1948. Out of the 58 member states at the time, 48 voted in favor, none against, with eight abstentions and two absentees. This date is now celebrated annually as Human Rights Day.

The Structure and Significance of the Declaration

Preamble:

Discuss the preamble of the UDHR, which sets the tone by acknowledging the inherent dignity and equal and inalienable rights of all members of the human family as the foundation of freedom, justice, and peace in the world.

The 30 Articles of the UDHR

Article 1:

All human beings are born free and equal in dignity and rights.

Article 2:

Everyone is entitled to all the rights and freedoms set forth in this Declaration, without distinction of any kind.

Article 3:

Everyone has the right to life, liberty, and security of person.

Article 4:

No one shall be held in slavery or servitude.

Article 5:

No one shall be subjected to torture or to cruel, inhuman, or degrading treatment or punishment.

Article 6:

Everyone has the right to recognition everywhere as a person before the law.

Article 7:

All are equal before the law and are entitled without any discrimination to equal protection of the law.

Article 8:

Everyone has the right to an effective remedy by the competent national tribunals for acts violating the fundamental rights granted by the constitution or by law.

Article 9:

No one shall be subjected to arbitrary arrest, detention, or exile.

Article 10:

Everyone is entitled in full equality to a fair and public hearing by an independent and impartial tribunal.

Article 11:

Everyone charged with a penal offense has the right to be presumed innocent until proven guilty.

Article 12:

No one shall be subjected to arbitrary interference with their privacy, family, home, or correspondence.

Article 13:

Everyone has the right to freedom of movement and residence within the borders of each state.

Article 14:

Everyone has the right to seek asylum from persecution.

Article 15:

Everyone has the right to a nationality.

Article 16:

Men and women of full age have the right to marry and to found a family.

Article 17:

Everyone has the right to own property.

Article 18:

Everyone has the right to freedom of thought, conscience, and religion.

Article 19:

Everyone has the right to freedom of opinion and expression.

Article 20:

Everyone has the right to peaceful assembly and association.

Article 21:

Everyone has the right to take part in the government of their country.

Article 22:

Everyone has the right to social security.

Article 23:

Everyone has the right to work, to free choice of employment, and to just and favorable conditions of work.

Article 24:

Everyone has the right to rest and leisure.

Article 25:

Everyone has the right to an adequate standard of living, including food, clothing, housing, and medical care.

Article 26:

Everyone has the right to education.

Article 27:

Everyone has the right to participate in the cultural life of the community.

Article 28:

Everyone is entitled to a social and international order in which the rights and freedoms set forth in this Declaration can be fully realized.

Article 29:

Everyone has duties to the community in which alone the free and full development of their personality is possible.

Article 30:

Nothing in this Declaration may be interpreted as implying for any State, group, or person any right to engage in any activity or to perform any act aimed at the destruction of any of the rights and freedoms set forth herein.

The Impact and Legacy of the UDHR

Explain how the UDHR has served as a foundation for international human rights law. It has influenced numerous national constitutions and laws, and it underpins many international treaties and conventions, such as the International Covenant on Civil and Political Rights (ICCPR) and the International Covenant on Economic, Social, and Cultural Rights (ICESCR).

Ongoing Relevance and Challenges

Discuss the ongoing relevance of the UDHR in today's world. While significant progress has been made, many challenges remain in ensuring that all people enjoy the rights and freedoms outlined in the declaration. Issues such as poverty, inequality, discrimination, and conflict continue to hinder the realization of human rights for all.

Conclusion: A Milestone for Humanity

Summarize the significance of the UDHR as a milestone in the history of human rights. It represents a collective commitment by the international community to uphold and protect the dignity and rights of every person. Conclude with a forward-looking statement about the need to continue striving for a world where human rights are respected and upheld for everyone.

Chapter 3
Civil and Political Rights

Introduction: The Essence of Civil and Political Rights

Begin by defining civil and political rights, explaining that these are the rights that protect individuals' freedoms from infringement by governments, social organizations, and private individuals. These rights ensure one's ability to participate in the civil and political life of society and the state without discrimination or repression.

Freedom of Speech

Definition and Importance:

Freedom of speech is the right to express one's opinions and ideas without fear of government retaliation or censorship. It is fundamental to the functioning of a democratic society, enabling the exchange of ideas and fostering an informed citizenry.

Historical Context:

Discuss key moments in history where freedom of speech played a crucial role, such as during the Enlightenment and the civil rights movements.

Real-Life Story:

Highlight the case of Nelson Mandela, who fought against apartheid in South Africa. Despite being imprisoned for 27 years, he continued to advocate for freedom and equality. His unwavering commitment to free expression and political activism ultimately led to the end of apartheid and the establishment of a democratic South Africa.

Freedom of Assembly

Definition and Importance:

Freedom of assembly allows individuals to gather peacefully for a common purpose, such as protests, demonstrations, or public meetings. It is essential for collective expression and advocacy.

Historical Context:

Discuss significant events like the Women's Suffrage Movement and the anti-Vietnam War protests, where freedom of assembly played a pivotal role.

Real-Life Story:

Focus on the Civil Rights Movement in the United States, particularly the 1963 March on Washington for Jobs and Freedom, where Dr. Martin Luther King Jr. delivered his iconic "I Have a Dream" speech. This mass gathering was instrumental in raising awareness and pushing for civil rights legislation.

Right to a Fair Trial

Definition and Importance:

The right to a fair trial ensures that individuals receive a fair and public hearing by an impartial tribunal. It is a cornerstone of justice, protecting individuals from arbitrary detention and ensuring that the law is applied equally.

Historical Context:

Explain the development of this right, referencing the Magna Carta and its influence on modern legal systems.

Real-Life Story:

Discuss the case of Mahatma Gandhi, who, despite facing numerous arrests and trials under British colonial rule, used the legal system to challenge unjust laws and advocate for India's independence. His nonviolent resistance and insistence on justice inspired movements worldwide.

Right to Privacy

Definition and Importance:

The right to privacy protects individuals from unwarranted intrusion into their personal lives by the government, corporations, or other individuals. It encompasses aspects like private communications, personal information, and home life.

Historical Context:

Discuss the evolution of privacy rights, especially in the digital age, where surveillance and data collection have become significant issues.

Real-Life Story:

Highlight the case of Edward Snowden, who exposed the extensive surveillance activities of the National Security Agency (NSA) in the United States. His revelations sparked global debates about privacy, security, and the balance between state power and individual rights.

Right to Vote (Suffrage)

Definition and Importance:

The right to vote allows individuals to participate in the democratic process by electing representatives and influencing government policies. It is fundamental to the principle of popular sovereignty.

Historical Context:

Trace the history of suffrage, including the expansion of voting rights to women, minorities, and other marginalized groups.

Real-Life Story:

Focus on the story of Emmeline Pankhurst and the British suffragette movement. Her relentless activism and the sacrifices made by suffragettes led to significant advancements in women's voting rights in the UK, inspiring similar movements globally.

Right to Freedom from Torture and Inhumane Treatment

Definition and Importance:

This right protects individuals from being subjected to torture or cruel, inhuman, or degrading treatment or punishment. It is essential for safeguarding human dignity and integrity.

Historical Context:

Discuss international efforts to combat torture, including the adoption of the Convention Against Torture.

Real-Life Story:

Highlight the story of Aung San Suu Kyi, who endured house arrest and severe restrictions in Myanmar for her political beliefs. Despite the harsh treatment, she remained a symbol of peaceful resistance and human rights advocacy, eventually contributing to the country's move towards democracy.

Freedom of Religion

Definition and Importance:

Freedom of religion allows individuals to practice, change, or abstain from religion without coercion or fear of persecution. It is fundamental to personal autonomy and cultural diversity.

Historical Context:

Discuss the role of religious freedom in the development of pluralistic societies.

Real-Life Story:

Mention Malala Yousafzai, who, while primarily known for her advocacy for girls' education, also stood up for religious freedom and the right to education against the Taliban's oppressive regime in Pakistan. Her bravery and resilience in the face of violence earned her global recognition and the Nobel Peace Prize.

Freedom of Movement

Definition and Importance:

Freedom of movement allows individuals to travel, reside, and work in any place of their choosing within the country and to leave and return to their country.

Historical Context:

Explore how restrictions on movement have been used as tools of oppression, such as during apartheid in South Africa or the Berlin Wall's division of East and West Germany.

Real-Life Story:

Highlight the plight of Syrian refugees fleeing conflict and seeking asylum in various countries. Discuss the challenges they face in exercising their right to seek safety and build new lives.

Conclusion: The Vital Role of Civil and Political Rights

Summarize the importance of civil and political rights in promoting individual freedom, justice, and democracy. Emphasize that these rights are interconnected and essential for the protection and empowerment of individuals.

Transition to the next chapter, which will explore economic, social, and cultural rights, highlighting how these rights complement civil and political rights in ensuring comprehensive human dignity and development.

Chapter 4

Economic, Social, and Cultural Rights

Introduction: Defining Economic, Social, and Cultural Rights

Begin by explaining that economic, social, and cultural rights (ESC rights) are essential components of human dignity and development. These rights ensure that individuals have access to basic necessities, opportunities for personal and professional growth, and the ability to participate in cultural life.

Right to Work

Definition and Importance:

The right to work guarantees everyone the opportunity to earn a livelihood through freely chosen or accepted work. It includes the right to just and favorable conditions of work, equal pay for equal work, and protection against unemployment.

Historical Context:

Trace the development of labor rights, from the Industrial Revolution to the establishment of international labor standards by organizations like the International Labour Organization (ILO).

Real-Life Story:

Highlight the struggle of Cesar Chavez and the United Farm Workers in the United States. Chavez fought for the rights of agricultural workers to fair wages, safe working conditions, and the ability to organize and bargain collectively. His efforts led to significant improvements in labor rights and inspired movements worldwide.

Right to Education

Definition and Importance:

The right to education ensures that everyone has access to free, compulsory primary education and accessible secondary and higher education. Education is crucial for personal development, empowerment, and the ability to participate fully in society.

Historical Context:

Discuss the global push for universal education, including key milestones like the Universal Declaration of Human Rights (Article 26) and the Education for All initiative by UNESCO.

Real-Life Story:

Share the story of Malala Yousafzai, a Pakistani activist for girls' education who survived an assassination attempt by the Taliban. Malala's advocacy has brought international attention to the importance of education for all children, particularly girls, and has inspired efforts to increase educational access in many countries.

Right to an Adequate Standard of Living

Definition and Importance:

The right to an adequate standard of living ensures access to essential needs such as food, clothing, housing, and medical care. It is fundamental for maintaining health and well-being and for living a life of dignity.

Historical Context:

Explore the development of social welfare systems and international efforts to combat poverty, including the United Nations' Sustainable Development Goals (SDGs).

Real-Life Story:

Discuss the impact of the Grameen Bank in Bangladesh, founded by Muhammad Yunus. The bank provides microloans to impoverished individuals, particularly women, enabling them to start small businesses and improve their living standards. This innovative approach has lifted millions out of poverty and promoted economic independence.

Right to Health

Definition and Importance:

The right to health encompasses access to timely, acceptable, and affordable healthcare of appropriate quality. It is essential for leading a life of dignity and for participating fully in society.

Historical Context:

Highlight the global efforts to promote health equity, including the establishment of the World Health Organization (WHO) and the adoption of the Alma-Ata Declaration on Primary Health Care.

Real-Life Story:

Share the story of Dr. Paul Farmer, co-founder of Partners In Health, an organization dedicated to providing quality healthcare to impoverished communities. His work in Haiti, Rwanda, and other countries has demonstrated the transformative impact of access to healthcare on individuals and communities.

Right to Social Security

Definition and Importance:

The right to social security ensures that individuals have access to support in times of need, such as unemployment, illness, disability, or old age. It is crucial for maintaining dignity and security throughout life.

Historical Context:

Discuss the development of social security systems, from early mutual aid societies to modern welfare states.

Real-Life Story:

Highlight the introduction of the Social Security Act in the United States in 1935. This landmark legislation provided financial support to the elderly, unemployed, and disadvantaged, significantly reducing poverty and insecurity for millions of Americans.

Right to Participate in Cultural Life

Definition and Importance:

The right to participate in cultural life ensures that individuals can enjoy their own culture, practice their religion, and use their language. It promotes diversity, creativity, and a sense of belonging.

Historical Context:

Discuss the role of cultural rights in fostering social cohesion and mutual respect, referencing key documents like the Universal Declaration of Cultural Diversity.

Real-Life Story:

Share the story of the Maori people's struggle for cultural rights in New Zealand. Efforts to revive and promote Maori language, arts, and traditions have strengthened their cultural identity and ensured their participation in the national cultural life.

Challenges in Realizing ESC Rights

Global Inequality:

Address the persistent issue of global inequality, which affects the realization of ESC rights. Discuss how economic disparities, discrimination, and lack of resources hinder access to these rights for many individuals and communities.

Case Study:

Highlight the situation in Sub-Saharan Africa, where poverty, lack of infrastructure, and political instability pose significant barriers to accessing education, healthcare, and an adequate standard of living. Efforts by international organizations and local initiatives are critical in addressing these challenges.

International Frameworks and Commitments

International Covenant on Economic, Social, and Cultural Rights (ICESCR):

Explain the significance of the ICESCR, adopted by the United Nations General Assembly in 1966. It commits signatory states to work towards the full realization of ESC rights.

Sustainable Development Goals (SDGs):

Discuss the SDGs, particularly those related to poverty, education, health, and inequality. These goals represent a global commitment to improving the quality of life for all individuals by 2030.

Conclusion: The Interdependence of Human Rights

Summarize the importance of ESC rights in achieving human dignity and development. Emphasize that these rights are interconnected with civil and political rights, and their realization is essential for holistic human progress.

Transition to the next chapter, which will explore specific rights related to women and children, highlighting the unique challenges and progress in these areas.

Chapter 5

The Right to Equality and Non-Discrimination

Introduction: The Foundation of Equality

Begin by explaining that the right to equality and non-discrimination is a cornerstone of human rights. It ensures that all individuals are treated equally under the law and have equal access to opportunities and resources, regardless of their race, gender, religion, or other characteristics.

The Importance of Equality

Definition and Importance:

Equality means that everyone is given the same rights and opportunities without any discrimination. Non-discrimination means that no one is treated unfairly because of their identity or personal characteristics.

Historical Context:

Discuss the evolution of the concept of equality, from early philosophical ideas to modern legal frameworks. Highlight how the struggle for equality has been central to many social justice movements throughout history.

Race and Racial Discrimination

Historical Context:

Discuss the history of racial discrimination, including slavery, colonialism, and apartheid. Explain how systemic racism has been embedded in societies and legal systems.

Landmark Cases:

Brown v. Board of Education (1954):

Highlight this U.S. Supreme Court case that declared state laws establishing separate public schools for black and white students to be unconstitutional. It was a major victory in the fight against racial segregation and a significant step towards desegregation.

Movements:

Civil Rights Movement:

Focus on key figures like Martin Luther King Jr. and organizations like the NAACP. Highlight major events such as the March on Washington and the Civil Rights Act of 1964, which outlawed discrimination based on race, color, religion, sex, or national origin.

Gender and Gender Discrimination

Historical Context:

Trace the history of gender discrimination, highlighting how women and non-binary individuals have faced inequalities in rights, opportunities, and treatment.

Landmark Cases:

United States v. Virginia (1996):

This U.S. Supreme Court case ruled that the Virginia Military Institute's male-only admissions policy was unconstitutional, reinforcing that gender-based discrimination must meet stringent scrutiny.

Movements:

Women's Suffrage Movement:

Discuss the global struggle for women's right to vote, focusing on leaders like Emmeline Pankhurst in the UK and Susan B. Anthony in the U.S. Highlight significant milestones like the passage of the 19th Amendment in the U.S. and similar victories in other countries.

#MeToo Movement:

Highlight this recent movement that has brought global attention to sexual harassment and assault, leading to increased awareness and changes in policies and attitudes towards gender-based violence.

Religion and Religious Discrimination

Historical Context:

Explain the history of religious discrimination, including persecution, forced conversions, and religious wars. Highlight how religious intolerance has led to conflicts and human rights abuses.

Landmark Cases:

Employment Division v. Smith (1990):

This U.S. Supreme Court case ruled that states could deny unemployment benefits to workers fired for using illegal drugs for religious purposes, prompting discussions on religious freedom versus state laws.

Movements:

Interfaith Movements:

Discuss efforts to promote religious tolerance and understanding, such as the Parliament of the World's Religions and initiatives by organizations like Religions for Peace.

Other Forms of Discrimination

LGBTQ+ Rights:

Discuss the history of discrimination against LGBTQ+ individuals, including criminalization and social ostracism. Highlight progress made, such as the decriminalization of homosexuality in many countries and the legalization of same-sex marriage.

Landmark Cases:

Obergefell v. Hodges (2015):

This U.S. Supreme Court case legalized same-sex marriage nationwide, affirming that the right to marry is a fundamental right for all.

Movements:

Stonewall Riots:

Highlight the 1969 Stonewall Riots as a pivotal moment in the LGBTQ+ rights movement, leading to greater visibility and advocacy for equal rights.

Disability Rights:

Explain the history of discrimination against individuals with disabilities, including exclusion from education, employment, and public life.

Landmark Cases:

Olmstead v. L.C. (1999):

This U.S. Supreme Court case held that individuals with mental disabilities have the right to live in the community rather than in institutions, under the Americans with Disabilities Act.

Movements:

Disability Rights Movement:

Discuss key events and legislation, such as the Americans with Disabilities Act (ADA), which prohibits discrimination against individuals with disabilities in all areas of public life.

International Frameworks and Commitments

Universal Declaration of Human Rights (UDHR):

Reiterate the UDHR's role in promoting equality and non-discrimination, particularly Articles 1, 2, and 7, which emphasize equality before the law and protection against discrimination.

International Convention on the Elimination of All Forms of Racial Discrimination (ICERD):

Highlight the significance of ICERD, adopted by the UN General Assembly in 1965, as a critical international treaty focused on eliminating racial discrimination.

Convention on the Elimination of All Forms of Discrimination Against Women (CEDAW):

Discuss CEDAW's role in promoting gender equality and addressing discrimination against women globally.

Convention on the Rights of Persons with Disabilities (CRPD):

Explain CRPD's importance in protecting and promoting the rights of persons with disabilities.

Ongoing Challenges and Future Directions

Persistence of Discrimination:

Address the ongoing challenges in eradicating discrimination, including systemic biases, cultural norms, and institutional barriers. Highlight the need for continued advocacy, education, and policy reforms.

Emerging Issues:

Discuss emerging issues in equality and non-discrimination, such as the intersectionality of different forms of discrimination, the impact of technology on privacy and equality, and the need for inclusive policies in a globalized world.

Conclusion: The Journey Towards Equality

Summarize the importance of the right to equality and non-discrimination in building a just and inclusive society. Emphasize that while significant progress has been made, the fight for equality continues, and it requires the collective efforts of individuals, communities, and nations.

Transition to the next chapter, which will explore specific rights related to freedom and personal security, highlighting their importance in ensuring individuals can live free from fear and coercion.

Chapter 6
The Rights of Children

Introduction: The Unique Rights of Children

Begin by explaining that children, due to their vulnerability and developmental needs, have specific rights that ensure their well-being, growth, and protection. These rights recognize that children require special care and assistance to thrive.

The Right to Education

Definition and Importance:

The right to education ensures that every child has access to free, quality primary education and accessible secondary and higher education. Education is vital for personal development, social integration, and economic opportunity.

Historical Context:

Trace the global efforts to promote universal education, including significant milestones such as the adoption of the Convention on the Rights of the Child (CRC) and initiatives like Education for All.

Real-Life Story:

Share the story of Malala Yousafzai, a Pakistani girl who advocated for girls' education despite threats from the Taliban. Her determination and activism brought global attention to the importance of education for all children, leading to her becoming the youngest-ever Nobel Prize laureate.

The Right to Protection from Exploitation

Definition and Importance:

This right protects children from all forms of exploitation, including child labor, trafficking, and sexual exploitation. It ensures that children can grow up in a safe and nurturing environment.

Historical Context:

Discuss the evolution of child protection laws, including the establishment of the International Labour Organization (ILO) conventions on child labor and the implementation of national and international child protection frameworks.

Real-Life Story:

Highlight the work of Iqbal Masih, a Pakistani child laborer who escaped bondage and became an advocate against child labor. Despite his tragic death at a young age, his legacy lives on through ongoing efforts to eradicate child labor worldwide.

The Right to Play

Definition and Importance:

The right to play recognizes that play is essential for children's physical, mental, and social development. It includes access to safe spaces and opportunities for recreation.

Historical Context:

Explain the recognition of the right to play in the CRC and its significance in promoting holistic child development.

Real-Life Story:

Share the example of playgrounds and community centers established in war-torn regions, such as those created by humanitarian organizations like UNICEF. These spaces provide children with a sense of normalcy, joy, and a chance to heal from trauma.

The Right to Health

Definition and Importance:

The right to health ensures that children have access to adequate healthcare, nutrition, and clean water. It is essential for their growth, development, and overall well-being.

Historical Context:

Discuss global health initiatives aimed at improving child health, such as vaccination programs, maternal and child health services, and efforts to combat malnutrition.

Real-Life Story:

Highlight the success of the Global Polio Eradication Initiative, which has significantly reduced polio cases worldwide and improved health outcomes for millions of children.

The Right to an Identity

Definition and Importance:

The right to an identity ensures that every child is registered at birth, has a name, nationality, and family ties. It is crucial for legal recognition and access to other rights.

Historical Context:

Discuss the importance of birth registration and the challenges faced in ensuring that all children have a recognized legal identity.

Real-Life Story:

Share the efforts of organizations like Plan International, which work to increase birth registration rates in remote and underserved areas, ensuring that children have legal recognition and access to essential services.

The Right to Family Life

Definition and Importance:

The right to family life ensures that children can grow up in a loving and supportive family environment. It includes protection from separation from parents, unless it is in the child's best interest.

Historical Context:

Discuss the role of international treaties like the CRC in promoting family unity and the establishment of child welfare systems to support vulnerable families.

Real-Life Story:

Highlight the work of foster care and adoption programs that provide children without families the opportunity to grow up in stable and loving homes. Share a success story of a child who found a forever family through these programs.

The Right to be Heard

Definition and Importance:

The right to be heard ensures that children have a voice in matters affecting them and can express their views freely. It is fundamental to respecting their dignity and promoting their participation in society.

Historical Context:

Explain the inclusion of this right in the CRC and its significance in promoting child participation in decision-making processes.

Real-Life Story:

Share the example of youth councils and forums where children and adolescents can express their opinions and influence policies affecting their lives. Highlight a specific initiative where young voices led to meaningful change.

International Frameworks and Commitments

Convention on the Rights of the Child (CRC):

Discuss the CRC, adopted by the United Nations General Assembly in 1989, as the most comprehensive international treaty on children's rights. Highlight its four core principles:

non-discrimination, the best interests of the child, the right to life, survival, and development, and respect for the child's views.

Sustainable Development Goals (SDGs):

Explain how the SDGs, particularly those related to health, education, and poverty, aim to improve the lives of children and ensure their rights are upheld.

Challenges in Realizing Children's Rights

Global Inequality:

Address the persistent issue of global inequality, which affects the realization of children's rights. Discuss how poverty, conflict, and lack of resources hinder access to education, healthcare, and protection for many children.

Case Study:

Highlight the situation in conflict zones, where children face heightened risks of exploitation, displacement, and interrupted education. Discuss the efforts of international organizations to provide emergency aid, education, and protection to affected children.

Ongoing Efforts and Future Directions

Advocacy and Awareness:

Emphasize the importance of continued advocacy and awareness-raising efforts to promote and protect children's rights. Highlight the role of governments, NGOs, and communities in these efforts.

Innovative Solutions:

Discuss innovative approaches to improving children's lives, such as technology-based education programs, mobile health clinics, and community-driven child protection initiatives.

Conclusion: The Future of Children's Rights

Summarize the importance of recognizing and protecting the specific rights of children to ensure their well-being, development, and dignity. Emphasize that children are the future, and investing in their rights is investing in a better world for all.

Transition to the next chapter, which will explore the rights of women, highlighting the unique challenges they face and the progress made in advancing gender equality.

Chapter 7
Women's Rights

Introduction: The Struggle for Women's Rights

Begin by explaining that women's rights are an integral part of human rights, aimed at achieving gender equality and ensuring that women can live free from discrimination and violence. The struggle for women's rights has a long history and continues to evolve as new challenges and opportunities arise.

Historical Context: The Evolution of Women's Rights

Early Beginnings:

Trace the origins of women's rights movements back to the late 18th and early 19th centuries, with early advocates like Mary Wollstonecraft, who authored "A Vindication of the Rights of Woman" in 1792, arguing for women's education and equality.

The Suffrage Movement:

Discuss the global movement for women's right to vote, focusing on key milestones and figures such as:

Susan B. Anthony and Elizabeth Cady Stanton:

Pioneers of the women's suffrage movement in the United States, who organized the Seneca Falls Convention in 1848 and co-founded the National Woman Suffrage Association.

Emmeline Pankhurst:

Leader of the British suffragette movement, who founded the Women's Social and Political Union (WSPU) and used militant tactics to demand voting rights for women.

Global Achievements:

Highlight major achievements such as New Zealand becoming the first country to grant women the right to vote in 1893, followed by other countries in the early 20th century.

Key Issues in Women's Rights

Voting Rights:

Explain the significance of the right to vote as a fundamental democratic right that empowers women to participate in governance and decision-making processes.

Case Study:

Highlight the passage of the 19th Amendment to the U.S. Constitution in 1920, which granted American women the right to vote, and similar achievements in other countries.

Equal Pay:

Discuss the ongoing struggle for equal pay for equal work, emphasizing that gender pay gaps persist globally.

Historical Context:

Trace the development of labor rights and anti-discrimination laws aimed at achieving pay equity, such as the Equal Pay Act of 1963 in the United States.

Real-Life Story:

Highlight the case of Lilly Ledbetter, an American woman who discovered she was being paid significantly less than her male counterparts. Her legal battle led to the Lilly Ledbetter Fair Pay Act of 2009, which strengthened workers' ability to challenge pay discrimination.

Reproductive Rights:

Explain the importance of reproductive rights, which include access to contraception, safe abortion, and maternal healthcare. These rights are crucial for women's health, autonomy, and ability to make informed decisions about their bodies and lives.

Historical Context:

Discuss the global movement for reproductive rights, including landmark cases and legislation such as:

Roe v. Wade (1973):

The U.S. Supreme Court case that legalized abortion nationwide, recognizing a woman's right to privacy in making medical decisions.

International Efforts:

Highlight the work of organizations like Planned Parenthood and the United Nations Population Fund (UNFPA) in promoting reproductive health and rights worldwide.

Real-Life Story:

Share the story of Dr. Rebecca Gomperts, founder of Women on Waves, an organization that provides safe abortion services to women in countries where abortion is illegal or restricted.

Influential Women Leaders

Historical Leaders:

Marie Curie:

A pioneering scientist who won Nobel Prizes in Physics and Chemistry, breaking barriers for women in science and academia.

Eleanor Roosevelt:

A key figure in drafting the Universal Declaration of Human Rights and a staunch advocate for women's rights and social justice.

Contemporary Leaders:

Malala Yousafzai:

A Pakistani activist for girls' education who survived an assassination attempt by the Taliban. She became the youngest-ever Nobel Prize laureate and continues to advocate for education and women's rights globally.

Ruth Bader Ginsburg:

A U.S. Supreme Court Justice known for her work in advancing gender equality and women's rights through landmark legal cases and decisions.

International Frameworks and Commitments

Convention on the Elimination of All Forms of Discrimination Against Women (CEDAW):

Discuss CEDAW, adopted by the United Nations General Assembly in 1979, as an international bill of rights for women. It outlines measures to eliminate discrimination and promote gender equality.

Beijing Declaration and Platform for Action:

Highlight the significance of the Fourth World Conference on Women held in Beijing in 1995, which produced a comprehensive plan for advancing women's rights and achieving gender equality.

Sustainable Development Goals (SDGs):

Explain how the SDGs, particularly Goal 5, aim to achieve gender equality and empower all women and girls by 2030.

Ongoing Challenges and Future Directions

Gender-Based Violence:

Address the persistent issue of violence against women, including domestic violence, sexual harassment, and human trafficking. Discuss efforts to combat these issues through legal reforms, education, and support services.

Economic Empowerment:

Highlight the importance of economic empowerment for women, including access to education, financial resources, and opportunities for entrepreneurship and leadership.

Political Participation:

Discuss the need for increased representation of women in political and leadership positions to ensure their voices are heard and their perspectives are included in decision-making processes.

Conclusion: The Future of Women's Rights

Summarize the progress made in advancing women's rights and the ongoing struggle to achieve full gender equality. Emphasize that the fight for women's rights is a collective effort that requires the support and participation of individuals, communities, and nations.

Transition to the next chapter, which will explore the rights of marginalized communities, highlighting the unique challenges they face and the importance of inclusive policies and practices.

Chapter 8

Indigenous Peoples' Rights

Introduction: The Unique Rights of Indigenous Peoples

Begin by explaining that indigenous peoples are the original inhabitants of regions around the world, with distinct cultures, languages, and traditions. Due to historical injustices, colonization, and ongoing marginalization, indigenous peoples have unique rights aimed at preserving their heritage and ensuring their well-being and autonomy.

Understanding Indigenous Peoples

Definition:

Indigenous peoples are communities that have historical continuity with pre-colonial and pre-settler societies. They maintain distinct social, cultural, economic, and political institutions.

Global Distribution:

Explain that indigenous peoples are found across the world, with significant populations in regions such as the Americas, Africa, Asia, and the Pacific. Mention examples like the Native Americans in the United States, the Aboriginal peoples in Australia, and the Sami in Scandinavia.

Historical Context: Colonization and Injustice

Colonial Impact:

Discuss how colonization led to the dispossession of indigenous lands, destruction of cultures, and imposition of foreign governance systems. Highlight the forced assimilation policies, such as residential schools in Canada and the United States.

Resistance and Resilience:

Emphasize that despite these challenges, indigenous peoples have shown remarkable resilience and have continuously fought for their rights, recognition, and preservation of their cultures.

Key Rights of Indigenous Peoples

Land Rights:

Explain that land is central to the identity, culture, and survival of indigenous peoples. Land rights include the right to own, use, develop, and control the lands and resources they have traditionally owned or used.

Historical Context:

Trace the history of land dispossession and the struggle for land rights, including landmark treaties and agreements.

Real-Life Story:

Share the story of the Maori in New Zealand, who have successfully negotiated settlements with the government to reclaim their land and resources through the Waitangi Tribunal process.

Cultural Preservation:

Discuss the right of indigenous peoples to preserve, protect, and practice their cultural traditions, languages, and rituals. This includes the protection of sacred sites and the right to maintain and develop their cultural heritage.

Historical Context:

Highlight the impacts of cultural assimilation policies and the efforts to revive and protect indigenous cultures.

Real-Life Story:

Highlight the efforts of the Navajo Nation in the United States to preserve their language through educational programs and media, ensuring that future generations can speak and maintain their native tongue.

Self-Determination:

Explain the right to self-determination, which allows indigenous peoples to freely determine their political status and pursue their economic, social, and cultural development.

Historical Context:

Discuss the various forms of indigenous governance and self-determination, from autonomous regions to tribal councils.

Real-Life Story:

Share the example of the Inuit in Canada, who have established the autonomous territory of Nunavut, allowing them greater control over their lands and governance.

International Frameworks and Commitments

United Nations Declaration on the Rights of Indigenous Peoples (UNDRIP):

Discuss UNDRIP, adopted by the United Nations General Assembly in 2007, as a comprehensive international instrument that enshrines the rights of indigenous peoples. Highlight key articles related to land rights, cultural preservation, and self-determination.

International Labour Organization (ILO) Convention 169:

Explain ILO Convention 169, adopted in 1989, which is a legally binding international instrument that addresses the rights of indigenous and tribal peoples, focusing on their right to participate in decision-making and maintain control over their own institutions.

Ongoing Challenges and Future Directions

Land and Resource Conflicts:

Address the ongoing conflicts over land and resources, including illegal mining, logging, and land grabbing. Discuss the importance of legal recognition and protection of indigenous territories.

Climate Change:

Explain how climate change disproportionately affects indigenous communities, threatening their livelihoods and traditional ways of life. Highlight the role of indigenous knowledge in climate adaptation and mitigation.

Political Participation:

Discuss the need for greater political representation and participation of indigenous peoples in decision-making processes at local, national, and international levels.

Stories of Indigenous Communities and Their Fight for Recognition and Justice

The Mapuche in Chile:

Highlight the struggles of the Mapuche people in Chile to reclaim their ancestral lands and protect their cultural heritage. Discuss their resistance against land dispossession and their ongoing legal battles for land rights.

The Standing Rock Sioux Tribe:

Share the story of the Standing Rock Sioux Tribe's protest against the Dakota Access Pipeline in the United States. Emphasize their fight to protect their water sources and sacred sites, and the global solidarity that their movement inspired.

The Sami in Scandinavia:

Discuss the Sami people's efforts to preserve their cultural identity and traditional reindeer herding practices in the face of modern challenges. Highlight their political representation through the Sami Parliaments in Norway, Sweden, and Finland.

International Advocacy and Solidarity

Indigenous Movements:

Highlight the role of indigenous movements and organizations, such as the Indigenous Environmental Network and the International Indian Treaty Council, in advocating for the rights and recognition of indigenous peoples globally.

Global Forums:

Discuss the importance of global forums like the United Nations Permanent Forum on Indigenous Issues (UNPFII), which provides a platform for indigenous peoples to voice their concerns and influence international policies.

Conclusion: The Path Forward for Indigenous Rights

Summarize the importance of recognizing and protecting the rights of indigenous peoples to ensure their dignity, cultural survival, and well-being. Emphasize that the fight for indigenous rights is a collective responsibility that requires ongoing commitment and action from all sectors of society.

Transition to the next chapter, which will explore the rights of people with disabilities, highlighting the unique challenges they face and the importance of accessibility and inclusion.

Chapter 9
The Right to Health

Introduction: Understanding the Right to Health

Begin by explaining that the right to health is a fundamental human right, essential for living a life of dignity. This right encompasses access to healthcare services, essential medicines, sanitation, and a healthy environment. It ensures that every individual can achieve the highest attainable standard of physical and mental health.

Defining the Right to Health

Scope and Components:

Discuss the broad scope of the right to health, which includes not only access to healthcare services but also determinants of health such as clean water, nutrition, housing, and safe working conditions.

International Recognition:

Explain how the right to health is enshrined in key international documents, such as the Universal Declaration of Human Rights (UDHR) and the International Covenant on Economic, Social and Cultural Rights (ICESCR).

Historical Context: Evolution of Health Rights

Early Efforts:

Trace the history of public health initiatives and the recognition of health as a human right, starting with early sanitation and vaccination programs in the 19th century.

Post-World War II Developments:

Highlight the establishment of the World Health Organization (WHO) in 1948 and its role in promoting global health. Discuss the Alma-Ata Declaration of 1978, which emphasized primary healthcare and health for all.

Key Aspects of the Right to Health

Access to Healthcare:

Explain that access to timely, acceptable, and affordable healthcare services is a core component of the right to health. This includes preventive, curative, palliative, and rehabilitative services.

Historical Context:

Discuss the development of healthcare systems and policies aimed at providing universal health coverage, such as the National Health Service (NHS) in the UK and the Affordable Care Act (ACA) in the US.

Real-Life Story:

Share the story of the Cuban healthcare system, known for its universal coverage and strong emphasis on preventive care, resulting in health outcomes comparable to those of wealthier nations.

Healthy Environment:

Emphasize the importance of a healthy environment in achieving the right to health. This includes clean air, safe drinking water, adequate sanitation, and safe living conditions.

Historical Context:

Trace the history of environmental health initiatives, such as the Clean Air Act and Clean Water Act in the US, which have significantly improved public health outcomes.

Real-Life Story:

Highlight the efforts to address the Flint water crisis in Michigan, USA, where lead-contaminated water posed severe health risks. Discuss the community activism and government interventions aimed at resolving the crisis and ensuring safe drinking water.

Global Health Issues

Infectious Diseases:

Discuss the impact of infectious diseases such as HIV/AIDS, tuberculosis, and malaria on global health. Highlight the efforts to combat these diseases through initiatives like the Global Fund and the President's Emergency Plan for AIDS Relief (PEPFAR).

Real-Life Story:

Share the success story of the HIV/AIDS treatment and prevention programs in Botswana, which have significantly reduced new infections and improved health outcomes through a comprehensive national response.

Non-Communicable Diseases (NCDs):

Explain the growing burden of NCDs such as heart disease, cancer, diabetes, and chronic respiratory diseases. Discuss the importance of addressing lifestyle factors, early detection, and treatment.

Real-Life Story:

Highlight the efforts of countries like Finland, which implemented comprehensive public health strategies to reduce cardiovascular diseases, resulting in improved life expectancy and health outcomes.

Maternal and Child Health:

Discuss the importance of maternal and child health as a priority in global health. Highlight efforts to reduce maternal and child mortality through initiatives like the Millennium Development Goals (MDGs) and Sustainable Development Goals (SDGs).

Real-Life Story:

Share the example of Rwanda, which has made significant progress in reducing maternal and child mortality through investments in healthcare infrastructure, community health workers, and vaccination programs.

Mental Health:

Emphasize the importance of mental health as an integral part of the right to health. Discuss the challenges of stigma, lack of resources, and the need for comprehensive mental health services.

Real-Life Story:

Highlight the efforts of countries like Australia, which has implemented national mental health strategies and support services to address mental health issues and promote well-being.

Global Health Initiatives

World Health Organization (WHO):

Discuss the role of WHO in promoting global health, setting health standards, and coordinating international health responses.

Global Health Partnerships:

Highlight the importance of partnerships such as GAVI, the Vaccine Alliance, and the Global Fund to Fight AIDS, Tuberculosis, and Malaria in mobilizing resources and improving health outcomes.

Universal Health Coverage (UHC):

Explain the concept of UHC, which aims to ensure that all individuals and communities receive the health services they need without suffering financial hardship. Discuss the progress and challenges in achieving UHC globally.

Challenges and Barriers to Health

Economic Inequality:

Address the impact of economic inequality on access to healthcare and health outcomes. Discuss the need for equitable healthcare financing and social protection mechanisms.

Conflict and Displacement:

Explain how conflict and displacement pose significant challenges to health, with refugees and internally displaced persons often lacking access to essential health services.

Climate Change:

Discuss the health impacts of climate change, including increased frequency of extreme weather events, vector-borne diseases, and food and water insecurity. Highlight the need for climate-resilient health systems.

Stories of Advocacy and Change

Grassroots Movements:

Highlight the role of grassroots movements and civil society organizations in advocating for health rights and driving change. Share examples such as Partners In Health, which works to strengthen healthcare systems in impoverished regions.

Innovative Solutions:

Discuss innovative solutions to health challenges, such as telemedicine, mobile health clinics, and community health worker programs. Highlight successful initiatives like the use of mobile technology to improve maternal health outcomes in Kenya.

Conclusion: The Future of the Right to Health

Summarize the importance of the right to health in ensuring human dignity and well-being. Emphasize the need for continued efforts to address global health challenges and achieve health equity for all.

Transition to the next chapter, which will explore the rights of people with disabilities, highlighting the unique challenges they face and the importance of accessibility and inclusion.

Chapter 10
The Right to Education

Introduction: The Importance of Education as a Fundamental Human Right

Begin by explaining that education is a powerful tool for personal and societal development. It empowers individuals, fosters critical thinking, promotes equality, and drives economic growth. As a fundamental human right, education is essential for the exercise of all other human rights.

Defining the Right to Education

Scope and Components:

Discuss that the right to education includes access to free and compulsory primary education, available and accessible secondary education, and higher education that is equally accessible to all based on merit.

International Recognition:

Explain that the right to education is enshrined in key international documents, such as the Universal Declaration of Human Rights (UDHR) and the International Covenant on Economic, Social and Cultural Rights (ICESCR).

Historical Context: Evolution of Educational Rights

Early Efforts:

Trace the origins of the recognition of education as a right, starting with early educational reforms in the 19th century aimed at making primary education compulsory.

Post-World War II Developments:

Highlight the establishment of UNESCO in 1945, which has played a crucial role in promoting education worldwide. Discuss the adoption of the Convention on the Rights of the Child (CRC) in 1989, which explicitly recognizes the right to education.

Key Aspects of the Right to Education

Access to Education:

Explain that access to education means ensuring that all children, regardless of their background, can attend school. This includes eliminating barriers such as economic constraints, gender discrimination, and geographic isolation.

Historical Context:

Discuss significant educational reforms and policies aimed at increasing access to education, such as the Education for All (EFA) movement and the Millennium Development Goals (MDGs).

Real-Life Story:

Share the story of Malala Yousafzai, a Pakistani activist who, despite being shot by the Taliban for advocating for girls' education, continued her fight and became a global symbol for the right to education. Her work led to the establishment of the Malala Fund, which supports education initiatives worldwide.

Quality of Education:

Emphasize that the right to education is not just about access but also about the quality of education. This includes trained teachers, adequate infrastructure, and a relevant curriculum that promotes critical thinking and skills development.

Historical Context:

Discuss efforts to improve the quality of education through teacher training programs, curriculum reforms, and the integration of technology in education.

Real-Life Story:

Highlight the work of Bridge International Academies, which operates low-cost private schools in Africa and Asia, using innovative approaches to improve the quality of education for children in underserved communities.

Inclusive Education:

Explain that inclusive education ensures that all children, including those with disabilities and from marginalized groups, can learn together in the same schools.

Historical Context:

Discuss the global shift towards inclusive education, including the Salamanca Statement and Framework for Action on Special Needs Education (1994), which calls for inclusive schools.

Real-Life Story:

Share the example of Lebanon, where inclusive education initiatives have been implemented to integrate children with disabilities into mainstream schools, supported by organizations like UNICEF and the Ministry of Education.

Global Efforts to Improve Access to Quality Education

UNESCO's Role:

Discuss UNESCO's efforts in promoting education for all, including the Global Education Monitoring (GEM) Report, which tracks progress towards achieving Sustainable Development Goal 4 (SDG 4) on education.

Global Partnerships:

Highlight the importance of global partnerships such as the Global Partnership for Education (GPE), which mobilizes funding and technical support to strengthen education systems in developing countries.

Education Initiatives:

Discuss major education initiatives like:

The United Nations Children's Fund (UNICEF):

Explain UNICEF's role in supporting education programs, particularly in emergency and conflict-affected areas, to ensure children continue their education.

The Global Education First Initiative (GEFI):

Launched by the United Nations, GEFI aims to put every child in school, improve the quality of learning, and foster global citizenship.

Challenges and Barriers to Education

Economic Inequality:

Address how poverty and economic inequality remain significant barriers to education, with many families unable to afford school fees, uniforms, and supplies.

Real-Life Story:

Highlight the efforts of the "Back to School" campaign in India, which provides scholarships and educational materials to children from low-income families, enabling them to continue their education.

Gender Discrimination:

Discuss how gender discrimination affects access to education, particularly for girls, in many parts of the world. Address cultural, social, and economic factors that contribute to this disparity.

Real-Life Story:

Share the example of the CAMFED (Campaign for Female Education) organization, which works to educate girls in Africa, providing them with the resources and support needed to stay in school and achieve academic success.

Conflict and Displacement:

Explain how conflict and displacement disrupt education, with millions of children around the world forced to flee their homes and miss out on schooling.

Real-Life Story:

Highlight the efforts of the United Nations High Commissioner for Refugees (UNHCR) to provide education to refugee children, including the establishment of learning centers in refugee camps and host communities.

Infrastructure and Resources:

Discuss the lack of infrastructure and resources in many parts of the world, including inadequate school buildings, lack of teaching materials, and limited access to technology.

Real-Life Story:

Highlight the work of organizations like Room to Read, which builds schools, libraries, and provides educational materials in underserved communities across Asia and Africa.

Stories of Advocacy and Change

Grassroots Movements:

Highlight the role of grassroots movements and community-based organizations in advocating for education rights and driving change. Share examples such as the Pratham organization in India, which works to improve literacy and learning outcomes through community engagement and innovative teaching methods.

Innovative Solutions:

Discuss innovative solutions to educational challenges, such as mobile classrooms, e-learning platforms, and community schools. Highlight successful initiatives like the Khan Academy, which provides free online education resources to learners worldwide.

Conclusion: The Future of the Right to Education

Summarize the importance of education as a fundamental human right and its role in achieving social justice, equality, and sustainable development. Emphasize the need for continued efforts to address barriers to education and ensure that every child has access to quality education.

Transition to the next chapter, which will explore the rights of workers, highlighting the importance of fair wages, safe working conditions, and the right to organize.

Chapter 11

Freedom of Expression and Information

Introduction: The Importance of Freedom of Expression and Information

Begin by explaining that freedom of expression and access to information are fundamental human rights essential for the functioning of a democratic society. These rights empower individuals to express their opinions, share ideas, and access information necessary for informed decision-making.

Defining Freedom of Expression and Information

Scope and Components:

Discuss that freedom of expression includes the right to seek, receive, and impart information and ideas of all kinds, through any media and regardless of frontiers. Access to information involves the right to obtain and disseminate information held by public bodies.

International Recognition:

Explain that these rights are enshrined in key international documents, such as the Universal Declaration of Human Rights (UDHR) and the International Covenant on Civil and Political Rights (ICCPR).

Historical Context: Evolution of Expression and Information Rights

Early Milestones:

Trace the origins of these rights back to early democratic movements, such as the Magna Carta (1215) and the Enlightenment period, which emphasized the importance of free speech and access to information.

Post-World War II Developments:

Highlight the inclusion of freedom of expression in the UDHR (Article 19) and the ICCPR (Article 19), and discuss the role of international organizations like UNESCO in promoting these rights globally.

Key Aspects of Freedom of Expression and Information

Freedom of Speech and Opinion:

Explain that freedom of speech allows individuals to express their thoughts, opinions, and beliefs without fear of censorship or retaliation.

Historical Context:

Discuss significant historical events that advanced freedom of speech, such as the abolition of censorship laws and the establishment of free press principles.

Real-Life Story:

Share the story of Martin Luther King Jr. and his famous "I Have a Dream" speech, which exemplified the power of free expression in advocating for civil rights and social justice.

Access to Information:

Emphasize the importance of access to information in promoting transparency, accountability, and informed citizenship. This includes the right to access government records, public data, and independent media.

Historical Context:

Discuss the development of freedom of information laws, such as the Freedom of Information Act (FOIA) in the United States, which allows citizens to request and obtain information from public authorities.

Real-Life Story:

Highlight the efforts of investigative journalists like Woodward and Bernstein, whose access to information and reporting on the Watergate scandal led to significant political accountability and reforms.

Media and Internet:

Explain the role of the media and the internet in disseminating information, providing platforms for expression, and facilitating public discourse.

Historical Context:

Discuss the evolution of the media landscape, from traditional print and broadcast media to digital and social media, and their impact on freedom of expression and information.

Real-Life Story:

Share the example of platforms like Twitter and Facebook, which have been used for social movements such as the Arab Spring, where citizens utilized social media to organize protests and share information in the face of oppressive regimes.

The Role of Media and Journalists

Independent Journalism:

Highlight the importance of independent journalism in providing accurate, unbiased information, holding power to account, and serving the public interest.

Historical Context:

Discuss the role of landmark media institutions, such as The New York Times and The Guardian, in investigative journalism and exposing corruption and human rights abuses.

Real-Life Story:

Share the story of Maria Ressa, a Filipino journalist and CEO of Rappler, who has faced harassment and legal battles for her work in exposing government corruption and human rights violations in the Philippines.

Challenges Faced by Journalists and Activists:

Address the challenges faced by journalists and activists, including censorship, harassment, violence, and imprisonment. Highlight the importance of protecting these individuals to ensure the free flow of information.

Historical Context:

Discuss instances where journalists have been targeted for their work, such as the murder of Jamal Khashoggi, and the global response advocating for press freedom and justice.

Real-Life Story:

Highlight organizations like Reporters Without Borders (RSF) and the Committee to Protect Journalists (CPJ), which advocate for press freedom and provide support to journalists facing threats and persecution.

Global Efforts to Protect Freedom of Expression and Information

International Organizations:

Discuss the role of international organizations, such as UNESCO and the United Nations, in promoting and protecting freedom of expression and access to information.

Historical Context:

Highlight initiatives like the World Press Freedom Day, established by UNESCO, to raise awareness about the importance of press freedom and honor journalists who have lost their lives in the pursuit of truth.

Legal Frameworks and Treaties:

Explain the significance of legal frameworks and treaties that protect freedom of expression and access to information, such as the International Covenant on Civil and Political Rights (ICCPR) and regional human rights instruments.

Historical Context:

Discuss the adoption and implementation of these legal instruments and their impact on safeguarding these rights globally.

Real-Life Story:

Share the example of the European Court of Human Rights, which has issued landmark rulings protecting freedom of expression, such as the case of Handyside v. United Kingdom, affirming the importance of free speech in a democratic society.

Challenges and Barriers to Freedom of

Expression and Information

Censorship and Control:

Address the issue of censorship and control of information by authoritarian regimes, including internet shutdowns, media blackouts, and restrictive laws.

Real-Life Story:

Highlight the situation in countries like China, where the government employs extensive internet censorship and surveillance, and activists use innovative methods to circumvent these controls and share information.

Digital Divide and Access Inequality:

Discuss the digital divide and how unequal access to technology and the internet affects individuals' ability to exercise their right to information and expression.

Real-Life Story:

Share the example of initiatives like the One Laptop per Child program, which aims to bridge the digital divide by providing affordable laptops and internet access to children in developing countries.

Misinformation and Disinformation:

Explain the challenges posed by misinformation and disinformation, which undermine trust in media and information sources and threaten democratic processes.

Real-Life Story:

Highlight efforts by fact-checking organizations, such as Snopes and FactCheck.org, to combat misinformation and provide accurate information to the public.

Stories of Advocacy and Change

Grassroots Movements:

Highlight the role of grassroots movements and civil society organizations in advocating for freedom of expression and information. Share examples such as the Right to Information (RTI) movement in India, which led to the enactment of the RTI Act, empowering citizens to access government information.

Innovative Solutions:

Discuss innovative solutions to protect and promote these rights, such as encrypted communication tools, anonymous whistleblowing platforms, and citizen journalism. Highlight successful initiatives like WikiLeaks, which provides a platform for whistleblowers to share sensitive information anonymously.

Conclusion: The Future of Freedom of Expression and Information

Summarize the importance of freedom of expression and access to information in ensuring democratic governance, accountability, and human rights. Emphasize the need for continued efforts to protect these rights in the face of evolving challenges.

Transition to the next chapter, which will explore the right to privacy, highlighting its significance in the digital age and the measures needed to protect individuals' personal information.

Chapter 12

The Right to Privacy

Introduction: The Importance of Privacy in the Digital Age

Begin by explaining that the right to privacy is a fundamental human right crucial for the dignity and autonomy of individuals. In the digital age, where vast amounts of personal information are collected, stored, and processed, protecting privacy has become increasingly challenging yet vital.

Defining the Right to Privacy

Scope and Components:

Discuss that the right to privacy encompasses the protection of personal data, the inviolability of the home, and the confidentiality of communications. It also includes the right to be free from unwarranted surveillance and intrusions.

International Recognition:

Explain that the right to privacy is enshrined in key international documents, such as the Universal Declaration of Human Rights (UDHR) (Article 12) and the International Covenant on Civil and Political Rights (ICCPR) (Article 17).

Historical Context: Evolution of Privacy Rights

Early Developments:

Trace the origins of privacy rights to early legal traditions that recognized the inviolability of the home and personal correspondence. Discuss the impact of technological advancements, such as the invention of the telephone and the rise of mass media, on privacy concerns.

Post-World War II Developments:

Highlight the inclusion of privacy rights in the UDHR and ICCPR, and the establishment of legal frameworks in various countries to protect personal data and privacy.

Key Aspects of the Right to Privacy

Data Protection:

Explain the importance of data protection in safeguarding individuals' personal information from unauthorized access, use, and disclosure. Discuss the principles of data protection, such as consent, purpose limitation, data minimization, and security.

Historical Context:

Discuss the development of data protection laws, such as the European Union's General Data Protection Regulation (GDPR), which sets stringent standards for data privacy and security.

Real-Life Story:

Share the example of the Cambridge Analytica scandal, where the misuse of personal data for political profiling and targeted advertising highlighted the need for robust data protection measures.

Surveillance and Intrusions:

Address the issue of surveillance, both by governments and private entities, and its impact on privacy. Discuss the balance between security and privacy, particularly in the context of national security and law enforcement.

Historical Context:

Highlight historical instances of surveillance, such as the FBI's COINTELPRO program, which targeted civil rights activists, and the global surveillance disclosures by Edward Snowden in 2013.

Real-Life Story:

Share the story of Edward Snowden, a former NSA contractor who exposed the extent of global surveillance programs, sparking a global debate on privacy and leading to reforms in surveillance practices.

Digital Privacy:

Emphasize the challenges of protecting privacy in the digital age, where digital devices, online services, and social media platforms collect vast amounts of personal data. Discuss issues such as tracking, profiling, and data breaches.

Historical Context:

Discuss the evolution of digital privacy concerns, from the early days of the internet to the rise of big tech companies and the increasing use of artificial intelligence and machine learning.

Real-Life Story:

Highlight the efforts of digital rights organizations, such as the Electronic Frontier Foundation (EFF), which advocate for digital privacy and challenge practices that undermine users' privacy online.

Global Efforts to Protect Privacy

International Organizations:

Discuss the role of international organizations, such as the United Nations and the Council of Europe, in promoting and protecting privacy rights.

Historical Context:

Highlight initiatives like the Council of Europe's Convention 108, the first binding international treaty on data protection, and the establishment of the UN Special Rapporteur on the right to privacy.

Real-Life Story:

Share the example of the European Court of Human Rights, which has issued landmark rulings protecting privacy, such as the case of Klass and Others v. Germany, affirming the right to privacy against unlawful surveillance.

Legal Frameworks and Treaties:

Explain the significance of legal frameworks and treaties that protect privacy, such as the GDPR, the ePrivacy Directive, and national data protection laws.

Historical Context:

Discuss the adoption and implementation of these legal instruments and their impact on safeguarding privacy globally.

Real-Life Story:

Highlight the implementation of the GDPR in the European Union, which has strengthened privacy protections for individuals and set a global standard for data protection.

Challenges and Barriers to Privacy

Technological Advancements:

Address the challenges posed by technological advancements, such as artificial intelligence, biometrics, and the Internet of Things (IoT), which raise new privacy concerns.

Real-Life Story:

Share the example of facial recognition technology, which has been used by law enforcement agencies for surveillance, raising concerns about privacy and civil liberties.

Global Surveillance and Data Sharing:

Discuss the issue of global surveillance and data sharing between governments and private companies, and its impact on privacy.

Real-Life Story:

Highlight the revelations of the PRISM program, where major tech companies were compelled to provide user data to the US government, sparking global outrage and calls for greater transparency and accountability.

Digital Divide and Access Inequality:

Explain how the digital divide and access inequality affect individuals' ability to protect their privacy online, with marginalized communities often facing greater risks.

Real-Life Story:

Share the example of initiatives like the Internet Society's Beyond the Net Program, which works to bridge the digital divide and empower communities to protect their privacy and rights online.

Stories of Advocacy and Change

Grassroots Movements:

Highlight the role of grassroots movements and civil society organizations in advocating for privacy rights. Share examples such as the Privacy International organization, which works to protect privacy and challenge surveillance practices worldwide.

Innovative Solutions:

Discuss innovative solutions to privacy challenges, such as encryption technologies, privacy-enhancing tools, and decentralized platforms. Highlight successful initiatives like

Signal, an encrypted messaging app that provides secure communication for users.

Conclusion: The Future of Privacy Rights

Summarize the importance of privacy as a fundamental human right and its role in protecting individual autonomy, dignity, and freedom. Emphasize the need for continued efforts to address privacy challenges in the digital age and ensure robust protections for personal data and communications.

Transition to the next chapter, which will explore the right to work, highlighting the importance of fair wages, safe working conditions, and the right to organize.

Chapter 13
The Right to Work and Fair Conditions

Introduction: The Significance of the Right to Work and Fair Conditions

Begin by explaining that the right to work and fair labor conditions is a fundamental human right essential for ensuring economic stability, personal dignity, and social inclusion. This right includes the opportunity to earn a livelihood through freely chosen or accepted work and to enjoy just and favorable conditions of work.

Defining the Right to Work and Fair Conditions

Scope and Components:

Discuss that the right to work encompasses the right to access employment without discrimination, to receive fair wages, and to work in safe and healthy conditions. It also includes the right to rest, leisure, and reasonable limitations on working hours.

International Recognition:

Explain that these rights are enshrined in key international documents, such as the Universal Declaration of Human Rights (UDHR) (Article 23) and the International Covenant on Economic, Social, and Cultural Rights (ICESCR) (Articles 6-8).

Historical Context: Evolution of Labor Rights

Early Developments:

Trace the origins of labor rights back to the Industrial Revolution, when the rise of factory work led to exploitative labor practices, prompting calls for reform. Discuss the formation of labor unions and early labor movements advocating for workers' rights.

Post-World War II Developments:

Highlight the establishment of the International Labour Organization (ILO) in 1919 and its role in setting international labor standards. Discuss the inclusion of labor rights in the UDHR and ICESCR, and the development of national labor laws.

Key Aspects of the Right to Work and Fair Conditions

Minimum Wage:

Explain the importance of a minimum wage in ensuring that workers receive fair compensation for their labor, enabling them to meet their basic needs and support their families.

Historical Context:

Discuss the development of minimum wage laws, starting with New Zealand's introduction of the world's first minimum wage law in 1894, followed by other countries adopting similar legislation.

Real-Life Story:

Share the example of the "Fight for $15" movement in the United States, which advocates for raising the federal minimum wage to $15 per hour, highlighting the struggles of low-wage workers and the impact of wage increases on their lives.

Safe Working Environments:

Emphasize the importance of safe and healthy working conditions in protecting workers from hazards and ensuring their physical and mental well-being.

Historical Context:

Discuss the development of occupational health and safety standards, including the establishment of the ILO's Occupational Safety and Health Convention in 1981.

Real-Life Story:

Highlight the Rana Plaza factory collapse in Bangladesh in 2013, which exposed the dangerous working conditions in the garment industry and led to global efforts to improve factory safety and workers' rights.

Fight Against Forced Labor and Child Labor:

Address the issue of forced labor and child labor, which violate fundamental human rights and exploit vulnerable individuals, particularly in developing countries.

Historical Context:

Discuss the global efforts to combat forced labor and child labor, including the adoption of the ILO's Forced Labour

Convention in 1930 and the Minimum Age Convention in 1973.

Real-Life Story:

Share the story of Kailash Satyarthi, an Indian children's rights activist who has rescued thousands of children from child labor and trafficking, and was awarded the Nobel Peace Prize in 2014 for his efforts.

Global Efforts to Protect Labor Rights

International Organizations:

Discuss the role of international organizations, such as the ILO and the United Nations, in promoting and protecting labor rights globally.

Historical Context:

Highlight initiatives like the ILO's Decent Work Agenda, which aims to promote job creation, rights at work, social protection, and social dialogue.

Real-Life Story:

Share the example of the ILO's Better Work program, which improves working conditions and competitiveness in global supply chains through collaboration with governments, employers, and workers.

Legal Frameworks and Treaties:

Explain the significance of legal frameworks and treaties that protect labor rights, such as the ILO Conventions, national labor laws, and regional agreements.

Historical Context:

Discuss the adoption and implementation of these legal instruments and their impact on improving labor standards and workers' rights.

Real-Life Story:

Highlight the implementation of labor reforms in countries like Germany, where the introduction of the Hartz reforms in the early 2000s improved job creation and working conditions.

Challenges and Barriers to Fair Labor Conditions

Economic Inequality and Exploitation:

Address the challenges posed by economic inequality and exploitation, which result in unfair labor practices, low wages, and poor working conditions for many workers.

Real-Life Story:

Share the example of migrant workers in the Gulf states, who often face exploitative labor conditions and lack legal protections, highlighting the need for labor rights reforms and better enforcement.

Informal Economy and Precarious Work:

Discuss the issue of informal and precarious work, where workers lack job security, social protection, and legal recognition, making them vulnerable to exploitation and abuse.

Real-Life Story:

Highlight the struggles of gig economy workers, such as ride-share drivers and delivery workers, who often face low pay, long hours, and lack of benefits, and the efforts to improve their working conditions through advocacy and regulation.

Global Supply Chains and Corporate Accountability:

Explain the challenges of ensuring fair labor conditions in global supply chains, where workers in developing countries often face poor working conditions and low wages.

Real-Life Story:

Share the example of the Accord on Fire and Building Safety in Bangladesh, a legally binding agreement between global brands and trade unions to improve factory safety and workers' rights in the garment industry.

Stories of Advocacy and Change

Grassroots Movements:

Highlight the role of grassroots movements and labor unions in advocating for workers' rights and improving labor conditions. Share examples such as the United Farm Workers (UFW) in the United States, which fought for better wages and working conditions for agricultural workers.

Innovative Solutions:

Discuss innovative solutions to labor challenges, such as fair trade certification, corporate social responsibility initiatives, and worker cooperatives. Highlight successful initiatives like the Fair Trade movement, which ensures fair wages and working conditions for producers in developing countries.

Conclusion: The Future of Labor Rights

Summarize the importance of the right to work and fair labor conditions in ensuring economic stability, personal dignity, and social inclusion. Emphasize the need for continued efforts to address labor challenges, improve working conditions, and ensure fair wages for all workers.

Transition to the next chapter, which will explore the right to housing, highlighting its significance in ensuring a safe and secure place to live and the measures needed to address homelessness and inadequate housing conditions.

Chapter 14

Environmental Rights

Introduction: The Emergence of Environmental Rights

Begin by explaining that environmental rights are a relatively new but increasingly recognized aspect of human rights. These rights emphasize the need for a healthy environment as a foundation for the enjoyment of other human rights, highlighting the interdependence between a clean, safe environment and the well-being of individuals and communities.

Defining Environmental Rights

Scope and Components:

Discuss that environmental rights include the right to a healthy environment, which encompasses clean air, safe drinking water, healthy ecosystems, and sustainable development. These rights also involve access to information, public participation in environmental decision-making, and access to justice in environmental matters.

International Recognition:

Explain that environmental rights are supported by various international documents and declarations, such as the Stockholm Declaration (1972), the Rio Declaration (1992), and more recently, the recognition of the right to a healthy environment by the United Nations Human Rights Council in 2021.

Historical Context: Evolution of Environmental Rights

Early Developments:

Trace the origins of environmental awareness to the mid-20th century, when industrialization and urbanization led to significant environmental degradation, prompting the rise of environmental movements. Highlight key events such as the publication of Rachel Carson's "Silent Spring" (1962), which raised awareness about the dangers of pesticides.

International Environmental Conferences:

Highlight significant milestones like the United Nations Conference on the Human Environment (Stockholm, 1972) and the Earth Summit (Rio de Janeiro, 1992), which laid the groundwork for integrating environmental protection into human rights frameworks.

Key Aspects of Environmental Rights

Right to a Healthy Environment:

Explain the importance of ensuring a clean and safe environment for the enjoyment of basic human rights, such as health, food, and water. Discuss the detrimental effects of environmental degradation on human well-being.

Historical Context:

Discuss the growing recognition of environmental rights through international treaties and national constitutions, such as the incorporation of the right to a healthy environment in the constitutions of over 100 countries.

Real-Life Story:

Share the example of the Flint water crisis in the United States, where residents were exposed to lead-contaminated water, highlighting the need for government accountability and the protection of environmental rights.

Impact of Climate Change:

Emphasize the far-reaching effects of climate change on human rights, including the right to life, health, food, water, and shelter. Discuss how climate change exacerbates existing inequalities and disproportionately affects vulnerable communities.

Historical Context:

Highlight international efforts to address climate change, such as the adoption of the Kyoto Protocol (1997) and the Paris Agreement (2015), which aim to limit global warming and reduce greenhouse gas emissions.

Real-Life Story:

Share the story of Pacific island nations like Tuvalu and Kiribati, which face existential threats from rising sea levels, illustrating the urgent need for global action on climate change.

Pollution and Human Rights:

Address the impact of pollution, including air, water, and soil pollution, on human health and well-being. Discuss how industrial activities, waste disposal, and the use of harmful chemicals contribute to environmental pollution.

Historical Context:

Discuss landmark cases and regulations aimed at reducing pollution, such as the Clean Air Act (1970) and the Clean Water Act (1972) in the United States.

Real-Life Story:

Highlight the Bhopal disaster in India (1984), where a gas leak from a pesticide plant resulted in thousands of deaths and long-term health consequences, underscoring the need for strict environmental regulations and corporate accountability.

Global Efforts to Protect Environmental Rights

International Organizations:

Discuss the role of international organizations, such as the United Nations Environment Programme (UNEP) and the Intergovernmental Panel on Climate Change (IPCC), in promoting environmental protection and sustainable development.

Historical Context:

Highlight the establishment of UNEP in 1972 and the creation of the IPCC in 1988, which provide scientific assessments and policy recommendations on environmental issues.

Real-Life Story:

Share the example of the Global Environment Facility (GEF), which funds projects aimed at addressing global environmental challenges and supporting sustainable development initiatives.

Legal Frameworks and Treaties:

Explain the significance of legal frameworks and treaties that protect environmental rights, such as the Aarhus Convention (1998) on access to information, public participation, and access to justice in environmental matters.

Historical Context:

Discuss the adoption and implementation of these legal instruments and their impact on empowering individuals and communities to protect their environmental rights.

Real-Life Story:

Highlight the success of the Aarhus Convention in promoting transparency and accountability in environmental decision-making across Europe and Central Asia.

Challenges and Barriers to Environmental Rights

Economic Development vs. Environmental Protection:

Address the challenges of balancing economic development with environmental protection, where short-term economic gains often take precedence over long-term environmental sustainability.

Real-Life Story:

Share the example of deforestation in the Amazon rainforest, driven by agriculture and logging, which threatens biodiversity and contributes to climate change, highlighting the need for sustainable development practices.

Environmental Injustice and Inequality:

Discuss the issue of environmental injustice, where marginalized communities often bear the brunt of environmental pollution and degradation, lacking the resources and political power to defend their rights.

Real-Life Story:

Highlight the struggles of indigenous communities, such as the Standing Rock Sioux Tribe in the United States, who protested against the construction of the Dakota Access Pipeline to protect their water sources and sacred lands.

Global Environmental Governance:

Explain the challenges of global environmental governance, where international cooperation and coordination are essential but often hindered by conflicting national interests and priorities.

Real-Life Story:

Share the example of the Montreal Protocol (1987), a successful international treaty to phase out ozone-depleting substances, demonstrating the potential for effective global collaboration on environmental issues.

Stories of Advocacy and Change

Grassroots Movements:

Highlight the role of grassroots movements and environmental activists in advocating for environmental rights and protecting natural resources. Share examples such as the Fridays for Future movement, led by youth climate activist Greta Thunberg, which mobilizes global action against climate change.

Innovative Solutions:

Discuss innovative solutions to environmental challenges, such as renewable energy technologies, sustainable agriculture practices, and conservation initiatives. Highlight successful projects like the reforestation efforts in the Great Green Wall initiative in Africa, which aims to combat desertification and restore degraded lands.

Conclusion: The Future of Environmental Rights

Summarize the importance of environmental rights in ensuring a healthy and sustainable future for all. Emphasize the need for continued efforts to address environmental challenges, protect natural resources, and promote sustainable development.

Transition to the next chapter, which will explore the right to housing, highlighting its significance in ensuring a safe and secure place to live and the measures needed to address homelessness and inadequate housing conditions.

Chapter 15
Refugees and Asylum Seekers

Introduction: Understanding Refugees and Asylum Seekers

Begin by defining refugees and asylum seekers. Refugees are individuals who have been forced to flee their home country due to persecution, war, or violence. Asylum seekers are people who have sought international protection and whose claims for refugee status have not yet been determined.

Defining the Rights of Refugees and Asylum Seekers

International Protections:

Discuss the key international documents and agreements that protect the rights of refugees and asylum seekers, such as the 1951 Refugee Convention and its 1967 Protocol. These instruments define who is a refugee, their rights, and the legal obligations of states to protect them.

Key Rights:

Explain the fundamental rights of refugees and asylum seekers, including the right to seek asylum, protection from refoulement (being returned to a country where they face serious threats to their life or freedom), access to fair and efficient asylum procedures, and rights to basic necessities like food, shelter, and healthcare.

Historical Context: Evolution of Refugee Rights

Post-World War II:

Trace the history of refugee rights back to the aftermath of World War II, when millions of people were displaced, leading to the establishment of the United Nations High Commissioner for Refugees (UNHCR) in 1950 to coordinate international efforts to protect and support refugees.

Cold War Era and Beyond:

Discuss the evolution of refugee movements during the Cold War and the subsequent decades, highlighting how conflicts, human rights abuses, and natural disasters have contributed to global displacement.

Key Aspects of Refugee and Asylum Seeker Rights

Right to Asylum:

Emphasize the right to seek and enjoy asylum from persecution. Explain the legal processes involved in seeking asylum and the challenges faced by asylum seekers in navigating these processes.

Historical Context:

Highlight landmark cases and significant moments in the history of asylum rights, such as the acceptance of Vietnamese "boat people" refugees in the 1970s.

Real-Life Story:

Share the story of a family fleeing conflict in Syria, seeking asylum in Europe. Discuss their journey, the challenges they faced, and the support they received from humanitarian organizations.

Protection from Refoulement:

Explain the principle of non-refoulement, which prohibits returning refugees to a country where they face serious threats to their life or freedom.

Historical Context:

Discuss the origins and importance of this principle in international refugee law.

Real-Life Story:

Highlight cases where refugees have been protected from refoulement, such as the Rohingya refugees fleeing persecution in Myanmar.

Access to Basic Necessities:

Discuss the rights of refugees to access basic necessities such as food, water, shelter, healthcare, and education. Explain how these needs are met by host countries and international organizations.

Historical Context:

Provide an overview of the global refugee camps and resettlement programs established to support refugees.

Real-Life Story:

Share the example of a refugee camp, such as the Dadaab camp in Kenya, one of the largest refugee camps in the world, and the efforts to provide essential services to its residents.

Global Efforts to Protect Refugees and Asylum Seekers

International Organizations:

Discuss the role of international organizations like the UNHCR, the International Organization for Migration (IOM), and various non-governmental organizations (NGOs) in protecting and assisting refugees and asylum seekers.

Historical Context:

Highlight significant international initiatives and agreements aimed at improving the protection and support of refugees.

Real-Life Story:

Share the story of the UNHCR's role in coordinating international efforts to support Syrian refugees in neighboring countries and beyond.

Legal Frameworks and Treaties:

Explain the significance of legal frameworks and treaties that protect refugees and asylum seekers, such as the 1951 Refugee Convention and regional agreements like the OAU Convention in Africa and the Cartagena Declaration in Latin America.

Historical Context:

Discuss the adoption and implementation of these legal instruments and their impact on enhancing refugee protection.

Real-Life Story:

Highlight the impact of the Cartagena Declaration, which broadened the definition of refugees in Latin America to include people fleeing generalized violence and massive human rights violations.

Challenges and Barriers for Refugees and Asylum Seekers

Host Country Policies and Attitudes:

Address the challenges posed by restrictive policies, xenophobia, and discrimination in host countries, which can hinder refugees' access to protection and integration.

Real-Life Story:

Share the example of refugees facing xenophobia and discrimination in Europe during the 2015 refugee crisis, highlighting the importance of inclusive policies and community support.

Lengthy and Complex Asylum Processes:

Discuss the issues related to lengthy and complex asylum procedures, which can leave asylum seekers in legal limbo for extended periods.

Real-Life Story:

Highlight the experiences of asylum seekers waiting for their claims to be processed in countries with overburdened asylum systems, such as the United States or Greece.

Economic and Social Integration:

Explain the challenges refugees face in integrating into new societies, including language barriers, lack of employment opportunities, and cultural differences.

Real-Life Story:

Share the story of a refugee who successfully integrated into their host community, such as a refugee entrepreneur who started a business and contributed to the local economy.

Stories of Advocacy and Change

Grassroots Movements:

Highlight the role of grassroots movements and advocacy groups in supporting refugees and promoting their rights. Share examples such as the Refugee Council and other local organizations that provide legal aid, social support, and advocacy.

Innovative Solutions:

Discuss innovative solutions to refugee challenges, such as community sponsorship programs, educational initiatives, and digital platforms that connect refugees with resources and opportunities. Highlight successful projects like the

"Refugees Welcome" initiative in Germany, which matches refugees with host families.

Conclusion: The Future of Refugee and Asylum Seeker Rights

Summarize the importance of protecting the rights of refugees and asylum seekers in ensuring their safety, dignity, and ability to rebuild their lives. Emphasize the need for continued efforts to address the challenges they face and promote their integration and well-being.

Transition to the next chapter, which will explore the right to housing, highlighting its significance in ensuring a safe and secure place to live and the measures needed to address homelessness and inadequate housing conditions.

Chapter 16
Human Rights in the Digital Age

Introduction: The Intersection of Technology and Human Rights

Begin by explaining how the rapid advancement of technology has transformed many aspects of our lives, including how we communicate, access information, and exercise our rights. Discuss the emergence of the digital age and its profound impact on human rights.

Defining Digital Rights

Scope and Components:

Define digital rights as the human rights that extend to the digital environment. These include the right to access the internet, freedom of expression online, privacy, and protection from cyber threats.

International Recognition:

Explain how digital rights are increasingly recognized in international human rights frameworks, with documents such as the Universal Declaration of Human Rights being interpreted to apply in the digital context.

Historical Context: Evolution of Digital Rights

Early Internet Era:

Trace the development of the internet from its origins in the late 20th century to the present day. Highlight how the internet has become a critical infrastructure for exercising various human rights.

Milestones in Digital Rights:

Discuss significant moments in the evolution of digital rights, such as the adoption of the United Nations General Assembly resolution on the promotion, protection, and enjoyment of human rights on the internet in 2016.

Key Aspects of Digital Rights

Right to Internet Access:

Explain the importance of internet access as a fundamental right, enabling individuals to participate in the digital economy, access information, and exercise other rights.

Historical Context:

Discuss efforts to recognize internet access as a human right, including initiatives by countries and international organizations to provide universal internet access.

Real-Life Story:

Share the example of Estonia, one of the first countries to declare internet access as a human right and implement nationwide internet access programs.

Digital Freedom and Expression:

Emphasize the right to freely express opinions online and access information. Discuss the role of digital platforms in facilitating freedom of speech and the challenges posed by censorship and misinformation.

Historical Context:

Highlight key events such as the Arab Spring, where social media played a crucial role in mobilizing protests and advocating for change.

Real-Life Story:

Share the story of activists using social media platforms to raise awareness about social and political issues, such as Malala Yousafzai's advocacy for girls' education.

Privacy and Data Protection:

Discuss the right to privacy in the digital age, including issues related to data protection, surveillance, and the use of personal information by governments and corporations.

Historical Context:

Explain the evolution of data protection laws and regulations, such as the General Data Protection Regulation (GDPR) in the European Union.

Real-Life Story:

Highlight the case of Edward Snowden, who exposed mass surveillance practices by the US government, sparking global debates about privacy and security.

Challenges and Threats in the Digital Age

Cyberbullying and Online Harassment:

Address the growing issue of cyberbullying and online harassment, which can have severe psychological and social impacts on victims, particularly children and vulnerable groups.

Real-Life Story:

Share the story of a victim of cyberbullying, discussing the impact on their life and the measures taken to address and prevent online harassment.

Digital Divide:

Discuss the digital divide, the gap between those who have access to digital technologies and those who do not, and how it exacerbates existing inequalities.

Real-Life Story:

Highlight efforts to bridge the digital divide, such as the One Laptop per Child initiative, which aims to provide affordable laptops to children in developing countries.

Misinformation and Fake News:

Explain the challenges posed by misinformation and fake news in the digital age, including their impact on public trust, democracy, and social cohesion.

Real-Life Story:

Discuss the role of fact-checking organizations and initiatives to combat misinformation, such as Facebook's partnership with independent fact-checkers.

Global Efforts to Protect Digital Rights

International Organizations:

Discuss the role of international organizations like the United Nations, the International Telecommunication Union (ITU), and various NGOs in promoting and protecting digital rights.

Historical Context:

Highlight significant international initiatives and agreements aimed at safeguarding digital rights, such as the UN's efforts to promote internet governance.

Real-Life Story:

Share the example of the Internet Governance Forum (IGF), which facilitates discussions on public policy issues related to the internet.

Legal Frameworks and Regulations:

Explain the significance of legal frameworks and regulations that protect digital rights, such as the GDPR, which sets a high standard for data protection and privacy.

Historical Context:

Discuss the adoption and implementation of these legal instruments and their impact on enhancing digital rights.

Real-Life Story:

Highlight the impact of the GDPR in improving data protection practices and empowering individuals to control their personal information.

Stories of Advocacy and Change

Grassroots Movements:

Highlight the role of grassroots movements and digital activists in advocating for digital rights and addressing online issues. Share examples such as the Electronic Frontier Foundation (EFF), which works to protect civil liberties in the digital world.

Innovative Solutions:

Discuss innovative solutions to digital challenges, such as initiatives to enhance digital literacy, improve cybersecurity, and promote ethical AI practices. Highlight successful projects like Mozilla's efforts to promote an open and accessible internet.

Conclusion: The Future of Human Rights in the Digital Age

Summarize the importance of protecting digital rights to ensure that technology benefits all individuals and supports the exercise of their human rights. Emphasize the need for continued efforts to address digital challenges, promote digital literacy, and safeguard privacy and freedom online.

Transition to the next chapter, which will explore the right to housing, highlighting its significance in ensuring a safe and secure place to live and the measures needed to address homelessness and inadequate housing conditions.

Chapter 17
The Role of
International Organizations

Introduction: Understanding International Organizations

Begin by explaining the concept of international organizations, which are entities formed by multiple countries to address global issues, promote cooperation, and uphold international standards. Emphasize their crucial role in promoting and protecting human rights worldwide.

Historical Context: The Emergence of International Human Rights Organizations

Post-World War II Era:

Trace the origins of major international human rights organizations to the aftermath of World War II, a period marked by the recognition of the need for a global framework to prevent atrocities and protect human dignity.

Founding of the United Nations:

Discuss the creation of the United Nations (UN) in 1945 and its foundational role in establishing international norms and standards for human rights, including the adoption of the Universal Declaration of Human Rights (UDHR) in 1948.

Key International Organizations and Their Roles

The United Nations (UN)

Structure and Function:

Explain the structure of the UN, highlighting key bodies like the General Assembly, Security Council, and specialized agencies such as the UN Human Rights Council (UNHRC) and the Office of the High Commissioner for Human Rights (OHCHR).

Human Rights Instruments:

Discuss the UN's role in developing and promoting key human rights instruments, including the International Covenant on Civil and Political Rights (ICCPR) and the International Covenant on Economic, Social and Cultural Rights (ICESCR).

Monitoring and Enforcement:

Describe how the UN monitors human rights through mechanisms such as the Universal Periodic Review (UPR), special rapporteurs, and treaty bodies. Highlight the importance of these mechanisms in holding countries accountable for their human rights obligations.

Real-Life Story:

Share a success story where UN interventions led to significant human rights improvements, such as the role of UN peacekeeping missions in protecting civilians in conflict zones.

Amnesty International

Mission and Activities:

Introduce Amnesty International as a global NGO focused on campaigning against human rights abuses. Discuss its core activities, including research, advocacy, and mobilizing public opinion through campaigns and petitions.

Impactful Campaigns:

Highlight some of Amnesty International's most impactful campaigns, such as those against torture, the death penalty, and for the release of prisoners of conscience.

Real-Life Story:

Share the story of a prisoner of conscience whose release was secured through Amnesty International's advocacy, demonstrating the power of global solidarity and public pressure.

Human Rights Watch (HRW)

Mission and Methodology:

Explain the mission of Human Rights Watch to defend the rights of people worldwide by conducting thorough investigations and reporting on human rights violations. Discuss HRW's methodology, including on-the-ground research, interviews, and detailed reporting.

Influential Reports:

Highlight influential reports by HRW that have brought attention to major human rights issues, such as the use of child soldiers, abuses in conflict zones, and government crackdowns on dissent.

Real-Life Story:

Share an example of how HRW's reporting led to concrete changes, such as policy reforms or international interventions to address human rights abuses.

Challenges Faced by International Organizations

Political Pressures:

Discuss the challenges international organizations face from political pressures, including resistance from governments and geopolitical tensions that can hinder their efforts to hold violators accountable.

Funding and Resources:

Explain the difficulties related to securing adequate funding and resources to carry out their missions effectively. Highlight how budget constraints can impact their capacity to respond to crises and conduct comprehensive research.

Access and Security:

Address the challenges of gaining access to areas where human rights abuses are occurring, particularly in conflict zones or authoritarian states. Discuss the risks faced by human rights defenders and investigators in these environments.

Real-Life Story:

Share the story of human rights defenders working in dangerous conditions, such as those in war-torn Syria or under oppressive regimes, highlighting their bravery and the importance of international support.

Global Efforts and Collaboration

Inter-Organizational Cooperation:

Emphasize the importance of collaboration between international organizations, governments, civil society, and local NGOs to effectively address human rights issues. Highlight examples of successful partnerships that have led to significant human rights advancements.

Historical Context:

Discuss notable collaborative efforts, such as joint initiatives to combat human trafficking or coordinate responses to humanitarian crises.

Real-Life Story:

Share an example of a collaborative project, such as the Global Alliance Against Traffic in Women (GAATW), which unites various organizations to combat human trafficking.

Capacity Building and Education:

Explain how international organizations work to build the capacity of local human rights defenders and educate the public about their rights. Discuss training programs, workshops, and awareness campaigns aimed at empowering individuals and communities.

Historical Context:

Highlight significant education and capacity-building initiatives, such as UN workshops on human rights for law enforcement officials and judicial personnel.

Real-Life Story:

Share the story of a successful capacity-building program, such as the UN's efforts to train human rights defenders in Africa, leading to strengthened local advocacy and protection efforts.

Stories of Advocacy and Change

Grassroots Movements:

Highlight the role of grassroots movements in advocating for human rights and how international organizations support these movements through resources, visibility, and advocacy at higher levels.

Historical Context:

Discuss the relationship between grassroots movements and international organizations, emphasizing their complementary roles in driving change.

Real-Life Story:

Share the story of a grassroots movement supported by international organizations, such as the anti-apartheid movement in South Africa and the role of global solidarity in its success.

Innovative Solutions:

Discuss innovative solutions and technologies used by international organizations to promote and protect human rights, such as satellite imagery to monitor abuses or digital platforms for reporting violations.

Historical Context:

Highlight key technological advancements and their adoption by international organizations to enhance their work.

Real-Life Story:

Share an example of how innovative technology has been used to document and address human rights abuses, such as the use of satellite imagery to monitor ethnic cleansing in Myanmar.

Conclusion: The Future of International Human Rights Advocacy

Summarize the critical role of international organizations in promoting and protecting human rights, highlighting their achievements and the ongoing challenges they face. Emphasize the importance of continued support, collaboration, and innovation to address emerging human rights issues in an increasingly interconnected world.

Transition to the next chapter, which will explore the right to housing, highlighting its significance in ensuring a safe and secure place to live and the measures needed to address homelessness and inadequate housing conditions.

Chapter 18
Human Rights Defenders

Introduction: The Guardians of Human Rights

Begin by defining human rights defenders as individuals and groups who promote and protect human rights through peaceful means. Emphasize their crucial role in advancing justice, equality, and dignity worldwide, often at great personal risk.

Historical Context:

The Emergence of Human Rights Defenders

Origins and Evolution:

Trace the historical emergence of human rights defenders, highlighting key moments and figures from various eras who have stood up against injustice. Discuss how the concept evolved alongside the development of human rights frameworks.

Recognition and Protection:

Explain the formal recognition of human rights defenders by international bodies, particularly the adoption of the UN Declaration on Human Rights Defenders in 1998, which provides a framework for their protection and support.

The Role and Importance of Human Rights Defenders

Advocacy and Awareness:

Describe how human rights defenders raise awareness about human rights abuses, advocate for policy changes, and mobilize public opinion. Highlight their role in giving a voice to the marginalized and holding authorities accountable.

Grassroots Movements:

Explain how human rights defenders often lead or support grassroots movements, working closely with local communities to address specific human rights issues and drive social change from the ground up.

Challenges and Risks Faced by Human Rights Defenders

Threats and Intimidation:

Discuss the various forms of threats and intimidation faced by human rights defenders, including harassment, surveillance, arbitrary detention, and physical violence.

Real-Life Story:

Share the story of Berta Cáceres, an indigenous rights activist from Honduras who was murdered in 2016 for her efforts to protect the environment and indigenous land rights.

Legal and Political Obstacles:

Explain how human rights defenders often face legal and political obstacles, including restrictive laws, criminalization of their activities, and lack of access to justice.

Real-Life Story:

Highlight the case of Nasrin Sotoudeh, an Iranian human rights lawyer who has been repeatedly imprisoned for her work defending women's rights and political prisoners.

Psychological and Social Pressure:

Address the psychological and social pressures, such as isolation, stigma, and the impact on their families and personal lives.

Real-Life Story:

Discuss the experiences of human rights defenders in repressive regimes, such as the struggles faced by Chinese activists like Liu Xiaobo, who was imprisoned and died in custody for advocating democratic reforms.

Inspiring Stories of Human Rights Defenders

Malala Yousafzai:

Share the inspiring story of Malala Yousafzai, who survived a Taliban assassination attempt to become a global advocate for girls' education and the youngest-ever Nobel Peace Prize laureate.

Impact:

Highlight how Malala's advocacy has brought international attention to the importance of education for girls and inspired millions worldwide.

Nelson Mandela:

Discuss the legacy of Nelson Mandela, who dedicated his life to fighting apartheid in South Africa, endured 27 years in prison, and became the country's first black president.

Impact:

Emphasize Mandela's role in achieving racial reconciliation and promoting human rights and equality, making him a global symbol of justice and resilience.

Aung San Suu Kyi:

Talk about Aung San Suu Kyi's long struggle for democracy and human rights in Myanmar, including her years of house arrest and her eventual election as a leader.

Impact:

Highlight her contributions to the pro-democracy movement and the challenges she faced, noting the complexities and controversies surrounding her later political career.

Wangari Maathai:

Highlight the achievements of Wangari Maathai, a Kenyan environmentalist and human rights activist who founded the Green Belt Movement and won the Nobel Peace Prize for her contributions to sustainable development, democracy, and peace.

Impact:

Discuss how Maathai's work empowered women, promoted environmental conservation, and inspired global efforts toward sustainability and human rights.

Global Efforts to Support and Protect Human Rights Defenders

International Mechanisms:

Explain the role of international mechanisms and organizations, such as the UN Special Rapporteur on the situation of human rights defenders, in monitoring, supporting, and advocating for the protection of human rights defenders.

Real-Life Story:

Share examples of how international pressure and advocacy have led to the release or protection of human rights defenders, such as the intervention that led to the release of journalist Maria Ressa in the Philippines.

NGOs and Civil Society:

Highlight the role of non-governmental organizations (NGOs) and civil society in providing support, training, and resources to human rights defenders. Discuss initiatives like Amnesty International's Urgent Action Network, which mobilizes global support for at-risk defenders.

Real-Life Story:

Share the impact of campaigns by organizations like Front Line Defenders, which provides practical support and protection for human rights defenders at risk.

Grassroots Initiatives:

Discuss grassroots initiatives and local support networks that offer protection, solidarity, and resources to human rights defenders within their communities.

Real-Life Story:

Highlight successful grassroots initiatives, such as community protection networks in Latin America that support indigenous and environmental activists.

Stories of Advocacy and Change

Grassroots Movements:

Highlight the role of grassroots movements in advocating for human rights and how human rights defenders support these movements through resources, visibility, and advocacy at higher levels.

Historical Context:

Discuss the relationship between grassroots movements and international organizations, emphasizing their complementary roles in driving change.

Real-Life Story:

Share the story of a grassroots movement supported by international organizations, such as the anti-apartheid movement in South Africa and the role of global solidarity in its success.

Innovative Solutions:

Discuss innovative solutions and technologies used by human rights defenders to promote and protect human rights, such as satellite imagery to monitor abuses or digital platforms for reporting violations.

Historical Context:

Highlight key technological advancements and their adoption by human rights defenders to enhance their work.

Real-Life Story:

Share an example of how innovative technology has been used to document and address human rights abuses, such as the use of satellite imagery to monitor ethnic cleansing in Myanmar.

Conclusion: The Future of Human Rights Defenders

Summarize the critical role of human rights defenders in promoting and protecting human rights, highlighting their achievements and the ongoing challenges they face. Emphasize the importance of continued support, collaboration, and innovation to address emerging human rights issues in an increasingly interconnected world.

Transition to the next chapter, which will explore the right to housing, highlighting its significance in ensuring a safe and secure place to live and the measures needed to address homelessness and inadequate housing conditions.

Chapter 19
Challenges and Controversies

Introduction: Navigating Complexities in Human Rights

Begin by introducing the notion that while the concept of human rights aims for universal dignity and justice, its practical application often involves navigating complex and contentious issues. Highlight the importance of understanding these challenges to foster a nuanced and effective approach to human rights advocacy.

Balancing Security and Freedom

Historical Context:

Explain the tension between security and freedom, which has been a persistent issue throughout history, particularly during times of crisis or conflict.

Post-9/11 World:

Discuss how the 9/11 terrorist attacks fundamentally shifted global perspectives on security and led to policies that many argue infringe upon civil liberties, such as the USA PATRIOT Act and increased surveillance measures.

Current Debates:

Highlight current debates over the balance between national security and individual freedoms, such as government surveillance, the use of facial recognition technology, and the rights of individuals versus collective safety.

Real-Life Story:

Share the case of Edward Snowden, who exposed mass surveillance practices by the NSA, sparking global debates about privacy, security, and government transparency.

Impact of Global Crises

Pandemics:

Examine how global health crises, such as the COVID-19 pandemic, have impacted human rights, including issues of healthcare access, freedom of movement, and economic inequality.

Healthcare Access:

Discuss disparities in healthcare access during the pandemic, emphasizing how marginalized communities were disproportionately affected.

Freedom of Movement:

Explain how lockdowns and travel restrictions, while necessary for public health, raised concerns about freedom of movement and the right to assembly.

Economic Inequality:

Highlight how the pandemic exacerbated economic inequalities, impacting the right to work, social security, and an adequate standard of living.

Real-Life Story:

Share the experiences of frontline healthcare workers who faced significant risks and challenges, illustrating the intersection of health rights and labor rights during the pandemic.

Conflicts and Wars:

Explore how ongoing conflicts and wars around the world continue to pose significant human rights challenges, including violations of international humanitarian law, displacement of populations, and the use of child soldiers.

Humanitarian Crises:

Discuss the humanitarian crises resulting from conflicts in regions such as Syria, Yemen, and Ukraine, focusing on the plight of civilians and refugees.

War Crimes and Accountability:

Address the difficulties in holding perpetrators of war crimes accountable, despite international mechanisms like the International Criminal Court (ICC).

Real-Life Story:

Share the story of Malak Al Shehri, a young Syrian girl who became a symbol of resilience and hope after documenting her experiences during the Syrian civil war.

Economic and Social Inequalities

Wealth Disparities:

Discuss the growing wealth disparities both within and between countries, and their impact on economic and social rights, such as access to education, healthcare, and housing.

Historical Context:

Provide historical context on economic inequality, referencing key periods such as the Great Depression and the financial crisis of 2008.

Real-Life Story:

Highlight the story of a community initiative in a developing country that successfully addressed issues of poverty and inequality through local empowerment and sustainable development practices.

Labor Rights:

Examine the ongoing struggles for labor rights in the context of globalization, including issues of exploitation, unsafe working conditions, and the gig economy.

Real-Life Story:

Share the story of Kalpona Akter, a labor rights activist from Bangladesh who has fought tirelessly to improve working conditions in the garment industry, highlighting the intersection of labor rights and economic justice.

Technological Advancements and Human Rights

Digital Privacy:

Explore the challenges posed by rapid technological advancements, particularly in the realm of digital privacy and data protection.

Surveillance and Data Mining:

Discuss the ethical implications of surveillance technologies and data mining practices by governments and corporations.

Right to Internet Access:

Address the emerging recognition of internet access as a fundamental human right, given its importance for education, employment, and social participation.

Real-Life Story:

Share the experiences of digital activists who have fought for internet freedom and privacy, such as those involved in the Arab Spring uprisings.

AI and Automation:

Examine the impact of artificial intelligence and automation on human rights, particularly in the labor market, privacy, and decision-making processes.

Bias and Discrimination:

Discuss concerns about bias and discrimination in AI algorithms and their implications for justice and equality.

Economic Displacement:

Address the potential for economic displacement caused by automation and the need for policies that ensure fair transitions for affected workers.

Real-Life Story:

Highlight the work of researchers and activists who are advocating for ethical AI and fair labor practices in the face of technological change.

Climate Change and Environmental Rights

Global Warming:

Discuss the human rights implications of climate change, including its impact on livelihoods, health, and displacement.

Environmental Justice:

Explore the concept of environmental justice and the disproportionate impact of environmental degradation on marginalized communities.

Youth Activism:

Highlight the role of youth activists like Greta Thunberg in raising awareness about climate change and advocating for sustainable policies.

Real-Life Story:

Share the story of an indigenous community fighting to protect their land and resources from environmental destruction, illustrating the intersection of environmental and human rights.

Political and Social Backlash

Rising Nationalism:

Examine the rise of nationalism and populism around the world and its impact on human rights, including increased xenophobia, racism, and discrimination.

Erosion of Democratic Norms:

Discuss the erosion of democratic norms and institutions in various countries, leading to concerns about the protection of civil and political rights.

Real-Life Story:

Highlight the story of activists in countries experiencing democratic backsliding, such as those in Hungary or Brazil, who are working to uphold democratic principles and human rights.

Freedom of Press:

Address the increasing threats to press freedom and the safety of journalists, emphasizing the essential role of a free press in protecting human rights and democracy.

Real-Life Story:

Share the experiences of journalists like Jamal Khashoggi, whose murder highlighted the dangers faced by those who seek to expose truth and hold power to account.

The Role of International Cooperation and Solidarity

Global Efforts:

Discuss the importance of international cooperation and solidarity in addressing human rights challenges, including the role of international organizations, treaties, and coalitions.

Success Stories:

Highlight successful international efforts to address human rights issues, such as the global response to apartheid in South Africa or the international climate agreements.

Real-Life Story:

Share the story of a successful international campaign, such as the efforts to ban landmines through the Ottawa Treaty, illustrating the power of global cooperation.

Conclusion: Navigating the Future of Human Rights

Summarize the key challenges and controversies facing the human rights field today, emphasizing the need for continued vigilance, innovation, and collaboration to address these issues.

Highlight the importance of education, awareness, and active engagement in promoting and protecting human rights in an ever-changing world.

Transition to the final chapter, which will focus on envisioning a future where human rights are universally respected and upheld, and the collective efforts required to achieve this vision.

Chapter 20
The Future of Human Rights

Introduction: Envisioning the Future

Begin by emphasizing the importance of looking forward in the human rights journey. Reflect on the progress made so far, acknowledging both achievements and ongoing challenges. Highlight the need for continued vigilance, innovation, and solidarity to ensure a just and equitable future for all.

Emerging Issues in Human Rights

Technological Advancements:

Discuss the rapid pace of technological change and its implications for human rights.

Artificial Intelligence and Automation:

Explore how AI and automation can both advance and threaten human rights, emphasizing the need for ethical guidelines and regulations.

Digital Privacy and Security:

Address concerns about digital privacy, data protection, and the potential for surveillance, stressing the importance of robust privacy laws and digital rights.

Real-Life Story:

Share an example of how technological advancements are being used positively to promote human rights, such as blockchain technology for secure voting systems.

Climate Change and Environmental Justice:

Examine the growing recognition of environmental rights and the intersection of climate change with human rights.

Impact on Vulnerable Populations:

Discuss how climate change disproportionately affects marginalized communities and the need for policies that address these inequalities.

Youth Activism:

Highlight the role of youth activists in driving global awareness and action on climate issues.

Real-Life Story:

Share the story of an environmental activist or community successfully advocating for climate justice, illustrating the potential for grassroots movements to effect change.

Global Migration and Refugee Crises:

Explore the complexities of global migration and the rights of refugees and asylum seekers.

Forced Displacement:

Discuss the factors driving forced displacement, including conflict, persecution, and environmental degradation.

Integration and Inclusion:

Highlight the importance of policies that promote the integration and inclusion of migrants and refugees into host societies.

Real-Life Story:

Share a story of a refugee or migrant who has overcome significant challenges to build a new life, emphasizing the resilience and contributions of displaced individuals.

Potential Solutions and Innovations

Strengthening Legal Frameworks:

Emphasize the need for robust legal frameworks at national and international levels to protect and promote human rights.

International Treaties and Conventions:

Discuss the importance of ratifying and implementing international human rights treaties and conventions.

Domestic Legislation:

Highlight the role of strong domestic laws in ensuring the protection of human rights and holding violators accountable.

Real-Life Story:

Share an example of a country that has successfully strengthened its legal framework to better protect human rights, illustrating the impact of legal reforms.

Inclusive and Participatory Governance:

Advocate for governance models that are inclusive, participatory, and responsive to the needs of all citizens.

Community Engagement:

Discuss the importance of involving communities in decision-making processes and ensuring their voices are heard.

Transparency and Accountability:

Highlight the need for transparency and accountability in governance to build trust and ensure the effective protection of human rights.

Real-Life Story:

Share a story of a community that has successfully influenced local governance through participatory approaches, demonstrating the power of civic engagement.

Education and Awareness:

Stress the critical role of education in promoting human rights and fostering a culture of respect and understanding.

Human Rights Education:

Advocate for the integration of human rights education into school curricula and public awareness campaigns.

Empowering Individuals:

Discuss how education empowers individuals to advocate for their rights and the rights of others.

Real-Life Story:

Share an example of a successful human rights education program that has made a significant impact on a community or society.

The Importance of Continued Advocacy

Grassroots Movements:

Highlight the vital role of grassroots movements in driving social change and holding authorities accountable.

Community Organizing:

Discuss how grassroots organizing can empower communities and amplify their voices.

Global Solidarity:

Emphasize the importance of global solidarity and support for grassroots movements, particularly in repressive environments.

Real-Life Story:

Share a story of a grassroots movement that has successfully brought about significant change, illustrating the power of collective action.

Role of Civil Society and NGOs:

Discuss the critical contributions of civil society organizations and NGOs in advocating for human rights and providing support to vulnerable populations.

Advocacy and Campaigning:

Highlight the importance of advocacy and campaigning in raising awareness and influencing policy changes.

Support and Services:

Discuss the role of NGOs in providing essential services and support to individuals and communities facing human rights abuses.

Real-Life Story:

Share an example of an NGO that has made a significant impact in promoting and protecting human rights, demonstrating the effectiveness of civil society efforts.

A Vision for a More Just and Equitable World

Universal Human Rights:

Reaffirm the vision of universal human rights, emphasizing the need for continued efforts to ensure that all individuals enjoy the full spectrum of their rights.

Intersectionality:

Discuss the importance of understanding and addressing the intersectionality of human rights issues, recognizing how various forms of discrimination and inequality intersect.

Empathy and Solidarity:

Highlight the role of empathy and solidarity in building a more just and equitable world, encouraging individuals to stand up for the rights of others.

Real-Life Story:

Share an inspirational story of a community or society that has made significant strides toward achieving a more just and equitable world, illustrating the potential for positive change.

Conclusion: The Path Forward

Summarize the key themes and lessons from the chapter, emphasizing the importance of continued advocacy, innovation, and solidarity in advancing human rights.

Reflect on the collective responsibility to protect and promote human rights, encouraging readers to take action in their own communities and beyond.

End with a call to action, inspiring readers to be part of the ongoing human rights movement and contribute to building a future where dignity, justice, and equality are upheld for all.

The End!